2
132

D1161207

CONTENT OF STUDENT-TEACHING COURSES DESIGNED FOR THE TRAINING OF SECONDARY TEACHERS IN STATE TEACHERS COLLEGES

By

JOHN GARLAND FLOWERS, Ph.D.

Teachers College, Columbia University
Contributions to Education, No. 538

Bureau of Publications
Teachers College, Columbia University
NEW YORK CITY
1932

Copyright, 1932, by TEACHERS COLLEGE, COLUMBIA UNIVERSITY

ACKNOWLEDGMENTS

For the stimulating atmosphere of Teachers College, Columbia University, the author acknowledges his debt of gratitude. He is obligated to many teachers of that institution who have provided delightfully challenging and stimulating situations in their classrooms.

The author wishes to express particularly his appreciation for the assistance given him in the preparation of this study by the directors of training and the training-teachers of more than one-half of the teachers colleges of the nation. Both groups gave unsparingly of time and effort in supplying data which form the main body of the dissertation.

Especially heavy is his debt to Professors Thomas Alexander, Edward S. Evenden, and Maxie N. Woodring, members of his dissertation committee, who have given sympathetic guidance throughout the study.

He is also grateful to many others who contributed in some measure to the completion of this work. Professors W. C. Bagley, Florence Stratemeyer, and Helen M. Walker, all of Teachers College, and President Harry A. Sprague of the State Teachers College at Montclair, New Jersey, gave kindly criticisms of the dissertation during the course of its preparation.

Finally, to his wife, Lora H. Flowers, and his son, John Garland, the author acknowledges his debt of gratitude for encouragement and for valuable help in tabulating and organizing the materials of the study.

J. G. F.

CONTENTS

Contents

vii

CHAPTER I

THE PROBLEM AND THE PROCEDURE

INTRODUCTION

Student-teaching has been an important part of the program for the professional education of teachers in this country from the beginning of the movement to the present time. The impetus given to this phase of the program came from the practices in European countries, particularly Germany.[1] That country was the first modern nation to develop a state-supported system of teacher-training and it included "practical experience"[2] in classwork as a part of the prescribed course. Indeed, this phase of the work is still recognized by the German educational leaders as essential to the training of all teachers, whether it be for the elementary or for the secondary school service.[3]

The founders of the normal schools in America included student-teaching as a part of the prescribed training. Samuel Hall[4] in 1823, James G. Carter[5] in 1824-25, Thomas H. Gallaudet[6] in 1825, Cyrus Peirce[7] in 1839, all of New England, were the early exponents of student-teaching. As the normal schools were established in other states, this policy was accepted by the newer schools and became an integral part of the teacher-training program.

Until 1860 the practical training given was largely observation and what we now term participation. But a new departure developed in 1860 at Oswego, New York. Edward A. Sheldon, Secretary of the Board of Education and Superintendent of Schools, proposed that a city training-school be established for

---

[1] Learned, W. S., Bagley, W. C., and Others, *The Professional Preparation of Teachers*, Bulletin Fourteen, *The Carnegie Foundation for the Advancement of Teaching*, p. 27.

[2] Luckey, G. W. A., *The Professional Training of Secondary Teachers*, p. 37.

[3] Alexander, Thomas, *The Training of Elementary Teachers in Germany*, p. 27.

[4] Norton, A. O., *The First State Normal School in America*, p. 19.

[5] *Ibid.*, p. 14.

[6] Gordy, J. P., *The Rise and Growth of the Normal School Idea*, p. 14.

[7] *Ibid.*, p. 19.

I

the training of the primary teachers of the city. Graduates of
the high schools would be admitted to this teacher-training course.
"One half of the time was to be given to a discussion of educational principles and their application to teaching the elementary
branches, and the other half to teaching under criticism."[8] The
school placed great importance on student-teaching. The estab-
lishing of a "practicing school" as a part of the organization de-
cidedly influenced other normal schools which were coming into
existence in several of the states in the union. The teachers trained
under Sheldon's plan were recognized as outstandingly good. They
were sought by other normal school principals as excellent normal
school teachers in the newly established schools.

The precedents set by these pioneer institutions have greatly
influenced the trends in the programs of teacher-training as they
were subsequently established in the other states. As the normal
schools expanded into two-year, three-year, and four-year institutions, their objectives changed to conform with the changing
schools in which the graduates would eventually serve. By degrees, the requirements for entrance were made more and more
rigid; the minimum requirements now being graduation from
high school.

The high school, as we now know it, was not in existence when
the first normal school was established. The English Classical
School for Boys began in Boston in 1821; its name was changed
to the English High School in 1835, but not until after the Civil
War did the high school movement develop to any extent. Changes
came rapidly, however. By 1890 the public high school was taking
on new life; its expansion was tremendous after this date. Nat-
urally, the great increase in enrollment in this new type of school
tended to raise the standards of the normal schools, for they were
now able to recruit their students from graduates of schools with
higher levels of achievement.

The supply of teachers for the new high school was secured
from the liberal arts colleges and universities during the early
years of its development. In fact, until within comparatively
recent years most of the supply has come from these sources.
The colleges and universities "came to regard it as important that
they train the teachers of the schools which prepared for college."[9] During the early years of the development of the high

[8] Dearborn, Ned H., *The Oswego Movement in American Education*, p. 13.
[9] Hall-Quest, Alfred L., *Professional Secondary Education in Teachers Colleges*, p. 5.

school the colleges were able to supply the demand, the normal schools considering it their function to train for the primary and elementary grades. But as the tremendous increase in enrollment came in the high school, there was a demand for more teachers to take care of this expansion. The principals and presidents of the normal schools were anxious to meet this demand; in fact, they quite freely stated that the normal schools should be expanded into teachers colleges that would serve the needs of the public-school service from the kindergarten through the high school. The *N.E.A. Proceedings* from 1900 to 1910 contain many discussions on the merits and demerits of normal schools and teachers colleges as suitable institutions to train high school teachers. An excerpt from the *Proceedings* of 1908 reveals the following resolutions:

Whereas, The public schools are the schools of the people;

Whereas, The public schools being the schools of the people, all factors in their organization are very clearly identified with the life of the people;

Whereas, The preparation of teachers is an important factor in the success of the schools, and in the development of civilization; and

Whereas, The normal schools have grown out of the thought, sentiments and opinions of the people, and are the direct expression of the will of the people,

Be it resolved:

1. That the state normal school make high school graduation, or equivalent, a basis for admission to the standard normal course;
2. That normal schools prepare teachers for the entire public service —elementary and secondary;
3. That the preparation of the elementary teachers be two years and of the secondary, four years;
4. That the normal schools establish well-organized departments of research work leading to the solution of problems affecting education and life.

. . . .

7. That the curriculum of the normal school should be broad enough in scope to touch all phases of special preparation demanded by the broadening curriculum of the public schools.

C. C. Van Liew, Chairman
David Felmley
Z. Snyder

Since 1910 there has been a pronounced advancement in the professional status of the normal schools, particularly within the past decade. During this period these institutions have increased their offerings by from one to three years, with a tendency to the four-year program leading to the baccalaureate degree in education in both elementary and secondary fields. Coupled with this growth in professional status there has been a tremendous growth in enrollment. The increase in enrollment in these institutions was 240 per cent during the decade beginning with 1910.[10]

The forces contributing to this rapid expansion were many. One of the most potent factors was the increase in enrollment in the public elementary and secondary schools. Reports of the United States Office of Education show that in 1890 the high school enrollment was 211,596; in 1910 it was 984,699; in 1920 it had reached 2,199,398; and today the enrollment has been estimated in excess of 4,000,000.[11] This increase in enrollment created a demand for large numbers of teachers and gave impetus to the newly organized teachers colleges. To meet this demand meant not only expansion in physical plants but a raising of standards. The curriculum of the new college must expand to include the subject-matter required for the training of high school teachers, and a technique of teaching must be developed suitable to the high school.

The professional aspect of the training of the high school teacher had been left entirely to the colleges and universities; now, a new institution was bidding for an opportunity to provide such training. Should it follow the methods and procedures of the college and university? Should it continue the same methods and procedures used by the normal schools in the training of elementary teachers? Or, on the other hand, should it develop its own technique, taking from both types of institutions that which seemed desirable and modifying such procedures to meet the requirements of the service?

For the most part, teachers colleges have been relatively free to work out their own plan. In some states, they have followed the lead of the universities and colleges in the type of training prescribed; in other states the traditions of the normal school have held over and influenced them tremendously in the work done; and, in still others, there has been a blending and modification of all these policies.

[10] Payne, Bruce R., "Twenty Years of Progress in the Service Rendered by Normal Schools and Teachers Colleges," *Proceedings of the N.E.A.,* 1928, p. 917.

[11] *Biennial Survey of Education,* United States Office of Education, Bulletin 16, 1926–1928, p. 147.

President David Felmley, of State Normal University, Normal, Illinois, speaking before the Centennial Conference on Teacher Training, held at Ball Teachers College in 1923,[12] urged that:

High school teachers should be trained in the same environment as elementary teachers. Both need the same love of children, the same knowledge of the problems of childhood and youth. Both need a comprehension of the entire scheme of education provided by our public schools. To educate these teachers in separate schools with different aims, methods, standards, and traditions results in a serious break in spirit, in method, and in the character of the work as the child passes to the high school. Furthermore, this separate training begets an exclusive educational caste. Our schools are already suffering from the presence of this cleavage between the professional aristocracy of the high school and the commonality of the grades.

The course in student-teaching in the state teachers college has been developed in a way somewhat similar to this course in the normal schools. As the normal schools grew into teachers colleges which now trained students for service from the kindergarten through high school, the student-teaching facilities in the campus schools and in the off-campus schools were expanded to include the high school in order to provide laboratory facilities for student-teaching activities.

In most of these institutions, the same director of student-teaching administers the program for both elementary and secondary student-teaching. Although there were slight modifications in the organization of student-teaching for the elementary and secondary divisions, the general plan is the same. To what extent the courses, on the different levels, are alike or are similar in content is not known. This study is concerned entirely with the content of courses in student-teaching organized for the training of secondary school teachers; a comparison and an analysis of the techniques and procedures of the two fields is not made.

THE PURPOSE

This study has a twofold purpose, namely: (1) to determine the content of the student-teaching courses in state teachers colleges that train for the secondary schools; and (2) to suggest, after an analytical study of present practices, certain means for

[12] *Proceedings, Centennial Conference on Teacher-Training,* 1923, Indiana State Normal School, Vol. XVII, p. 43.

the improvement of the program of student-teaching for prospective high school teachers.

THE PROBLEM STATED

In determining the content of such a course, three major questions present themselves, namely: (1) How are the teachers colleges organized to give professional training to prospective secondary school teachers? (2) How are the courses in student-teaching organized and administered to carry out the programs of training which the institutions have set up? and (3) In what activities does the student-teacher engage while pursuing the course in student-teaching?

THE PROCEDURE

The data were obtained from six sources: (1) directors of training (student-teaching); (2) training or critic teachers; (3) catalogues and descriptive materials published by the several institutions; (4) graduate students majoring in the field of teacher-training; (5) interviews with directors of training, supervisors and critics; (6) and personal visitation of a limited number of institutions.

The essential facts were secured principally by the questionnaire method. However, personal conferences with a representative number of specialists who are engaged in administering the program of student-teaching secured many valuable data, particularly with regard to the organization of the institutions' facilities for the course. Several of the directors of training sent syllabi and mimeographed descriptions of their courses which supplement the materials asked for in the questionnaire.

The questionnaire sent to the directors of training asked for detailed information on the following items:

I. The Institution

Size of student body being specifically trained for secondary school service

The extent of the course prescribed for the training of junior and senior high school service

Scholastic requirement made of the student as a prerequisite for pursuing the course

Means of eliminating students who are noticeably unfit for the profession

Background of the student-teacher when assigned to student-teach-
. ing

The extent of the facilities the institution provides for the work of
the course

The nature and extent of student-teaching activities in courses other
than student-teaching

II. The Organization of the Course Itself

Person or persons held responsible for the student-teachers' work

Number of students assigned to a training-teacher at any given time

Number of hours per week each student is engaged in the activities
of the course

College credit given for the course

Length of the course

Proportion of time given to:

Observation

Participation

Preparation

Teaching

Extra-class activities

Conferences, individual and group

Miscellaneous activities

Distinction made in the work required for the experienced and the
inexperienced student-teacher

Means of evaluating the student's efficiency

III. Activities of the Course

A. Activities Involving Class Instruction
   1. Planning subject-matter
   2. Selection and organization of subject-matter for instruction
   3. Recognition of pupils' interests, abilities, and needs in class
      instruction
   4. Other essential factors in class instruction
   5. Evaluating pupils' achievements
   6. General activities involved in teaching pupils to study
   7. Specific techniques in teaching pupils how to study
B. Activities Involving Classroom Management and Control
   1. Routine factors
   2. Activities involving pupil-student-teacher relationships
C. The Student-Teachers' Part in Extra-Class and Community
   Activities
   1. Extra-class activities
   2. Community activities

D. The Student Teachers' Growth
   1. Personal factors
   2. Professional factors

SCOPE OF THE INVESTIGATION

The normal schools and the teachers colleges in thirty-two of the forty-eight states train secondary teachers for the major subjects of the high school curriculum.   In a few states, however, such as the New England group, the normal schools are organized to train secondary teachers also for certain special fields, such as home arts, industrial arts, commercial arts, agriculture, music, and physical education.   This study, being confined to the techniques of teaching the so-called academic subjects, includes only the state institutions that provide exclusively academic training.   Data from thirty of the thirty-two states that train secondary teachers in subjects of this nature are included in this study.   Table I reveals the distribution of states and institutions from which these data were secured.

All the directors of training in those teachers colleges that train secondary teachers were asked to contribute information in regard to the organization and content of the student-teaching courses in the institutions they serve.   Fifty per cent of the directors of training responded to this request.   No response was received from Alabama and Indiana.   An examination of catalogues and other printed material of the institutions of these two states indicates that their courses in student-teaching are not unlike those of other states; hence, the data are not affected by this lack of full representation.

TABLE I

DISTRIBUTION, BY SECTIONS AND STATES, OF THE SOURCES OF DATA INCLUDED
IN THIS STUDY*

SECTION	NUMBER OF STATES	NUMBER OF STATE TEACHERS COLLEGES	NUMBER OF DIRECTORS OF TRAINING	NUMBER OF TRAINING TEACHERS
Northeastern States	5	18	12	39
North Central States	10	17	19	8
Southern States	11	27	17	39
Western States	4	7	7	14
Total	30	69	55	100

* See Appendix A for complete list of institutions represented.

CHAPTER II

FACTORS OF ORGANIZATION AND ADMINISTRATION AFFECTING THE CONTENT OF STUDENT-TEACHING COURSES

INTRODUCTION

A study of the organization of the institutions was made to determine the existing policies with reference to the place which the course in student-teaching has in the entire program of teacher-training. The objective in this phase of the study was to determine whether the elements of time allotments, facilities for student-teaching, and underlying philosophies held by the various administrative officers with regard to the value of the activities, influence the organization and content of the course in student-teaching. Some pertinent questions arise in this connection. Which activities are given the greatest emphasis? Are the actual number of hours of teaching (in full charge of the class) influenced by the facilities for student-teaching which are provided by the institutions? Will the activities of the course be confined to observation and participation because of the lack of equipment, or because of a point of view that such activities are as valuable as responsible teaching?

Some of the more important factors influencing the program of training are: personnel of those who administer the courses in student-teaching, service load of those actively responsible, provision for laboratory facilities, general college requirements, the nature and extent of student activities in courses other than those in student-teaching, and the coöperation of the various staff members in the student-teaching program.

A. HOW ARE THE INSTITUTIONS ADMINISTERED AND ORGANIZED FOR STUDENT-TEACHING?

PERSONNEL OF THOSE WHO ADMINISTER THE COURSE

The program of student-teaching in the state teachers colleges is administered either by a director of student-teaching or by the

9

head of the department of education, who, in addition, serves as the director of student-teaching. A study of the reports concerning the academic preparation of the fifty-five officers administering the student-teaching program showed that one-third hold the doctor's degree, and all except one hold the master's degree. This academic preparation is quite comparable to that of the other administrative officers and heads of other departments in these same fifty-five institutions.

The group of training-teachers coöperating, one hundred in number, represents a well trained body of teachers. All possess the baccalaureate degree, approximately one-half possess the master's degree, and one-tenth have done work leading toward the doctorate. Garrison's study[1] points out that the training-teacher is "well informed on modern educational theory and practice, by virtue of her training and experience, her frequent acceptance as a college instructor, her professional contacts in her daily work, and her continued and recent study in our better colleges and universities."

LABORATORY FACILITIES

It has been recognized by the leaders in the field of teacher-training that one of the most important factors in working out an effective program of student-teaching is the provision made for laboratory facilities for observation, participation, and teaching activities. Bagley, in Bulletin Number 14, *The Professional Preparation of Teachers for American Public Schools*,[2] states that the minimal requirement with regard to practice facilities should be the ratio of four pupils to one college senior student enrolled. The standards of the American Association of Teachers Colleges (1930) state that "for every eighteen college students to be given ninety hours of student-teaching, there shall be a minimum group of thirty children, either in the campus training school or in affiliated urban or rural schools under the supervision of the teachers college or normal school."

A study of the facilities of fifty-two of the institutions reported by directors of training replying to the questionnaire revealed significant facts with respect to ratio of pupils to student-teachers.

---

[1] Garrison, L. G., *Status and Work of the Training Supervisor*, p. 12.

[2] Learned, W. S., Bagley, W. C., and Others, *The Professional Preparation of Teachers for American Public Schools*, pp. 193-195. Carnegie Foundation for the Advancement of Teaching.

1. Of the fifty-five institutions, 34.6 per cent have laboratory facilities in a ratio of less than one pupil to one college senior.
2. The median institution in the distribution showed the availability of facilities in the ratio of two pupils to one college senior.
3. The distribution of ratios ranged from 0.2 pupils to one college senior, to 68.7 pupils to one college senior.

An analysis of those data relating to the facilities provided by the state teachers colleges indicates that twenty-nine of the fifty-two institutions considered provide off-campus facilities. Of these twenty-nine institutions, nineteen provide facilities with the ratio of four or more students in the training schools to one college senior enrolled in the institution; only three institutions without off-campus schools provide facilities equal to this ratio. It is clear that in those institutions providing off-campus training schools there is a tendency to provide more adequate facilities for the student-teaching program, if we accept the recommendation of Bulletin Fourteen and the standards of the American Association of Teachers Colleges.

THE SUPERVISORY LOAD OF TRAINING-TEACHERS

If the spirit of the standards of the American Association of Teachers Colleges, *1930 Yearbook*, is followed, not more than eighteen student-teachers should be supervised by a training-teacher during one given year. If this is divided into terms the training-teacher might supervise six student-teachers during one term; or if organized on the semester basis, she might supervise nine student-teachers at one given time. The American Association of Teachers Colleges standards[3] specify that a minimum of two-fifths of the time of classwork be taught by the training-teacher. Although this standard is evidently meant to safeguard the child's interests, and may lighten the teaching load, it does not reduce the load of supervisory responsibilities.

It is significant to note in Table II that the typical institution assigns four students to the training-teacher, but in one instance at least it was found that thirty students are frequently assigned to the training-teacher at one given time. This would mean that the high school teacher, in addition to teaching the children of the

[3] *American Association of Teachers Colleges, Standards for Accrediting Teachers Colleges*, Standard VII E. 1930.

classroom, would be taking care of five student-teachers during each class period.

TABLE II

RANGE AND MEDIAN NUMBER OF STUDENT-TEACHERS ASSIGNED TO THE
TRAINING-TEACHER AT ONE GIVEN TIME

	RANGE	MEDIAN
Maximum	1–30	6
Average	1–17	4
Minimum	1– 8	1

Number of institutions considered 48

REQUIREMENTS THAT INSTITUTIONS MAKE AS PREREQUISITE TO
THE COURSE IN STUDENT-TEACHING

There is no absolute proof to substantiate the assumption that academic preparation prior to the course in student-teaching directly affects the content of the course itself. It seems obvious, however, that the student cannot teach that which he does not know, and that if he is placed in a position in which he is required to teach material inadequately mastered, his task becomes one of mastering information rather than one of developing the skills of classroom teaching. The assumption is therefore made that the content of the course is conditioned by the academic preparation possessed by the student-teacher. The purpose of this section is to determine what preparation is required of students prior to their assignment to student-teaching activities.

The directors of training, by means of the questionnaire, gave information concerning the four following items: the amount of training required in the major and minor fields prior to assignment; the length of the college course preparing junior and senior high school teachers; the college year in which the student does student-teaching; and the amount of college credit given for the course.

Amount of Training Required in the Major and Minor Fields Prior to Assignment to Student-Teaching. This question has significance because it reveals the amount of specific academic preparation the student-teacher must have before entering definitely into the training experience of the course in student-teaching.

An examination of the data reported by the directors of training indicates that there is wide variation of practice in state teachers colleges in this regard. Approximately 20 per cent of the institutions make no requirement in the amount of preparation in the major field prior to assignment. Forty per cent of the institutions make no requirement in the minor fields. The general tendency is to require from twelve to twenty-four semester-hours of work in the major subject, although the range is from no requirement to forty-five semester-hours.

These data indicate that the typical student, prior to his course in student-teaching, has had little more than two years of academic preparation or has pursued one course for little more than two years on the college level in the subject-matter he teaches. The chances are great that he has pursued the minor subject prior to the student-teaching experience for no longer a period than one academic year.

TABLE III

NUMBER OF SEMESTER-HOURS THE STUDENT MUST HAVE COMPLETED IN
HIS MAJOR AND MINOR FIELDS AS A MINIMUM REQUIREMENT
BEFORE ASSIGNMENT TO STUDENT-TEACHING

SEMESTER-HOURS	MAJOR SUBJECT No. of Institutions	MINOR SUBJECT No. of Institutions
No requirement	10	16
8 to 11	4	11
12 to 18	11	15
19 to 24	11	6
25 to 30	11	6
31 to 36	6	1
37 to 45	2	0

Number of institutions considered 55

Length of the College Course Preparing Junior and Senior High School Teachers. Most of the teachers colleges provide a four-year course for the training of high school teachers. This is particularly true in the training of senior high school teachers, in which case 94.5 per cent offer a four-year course. In the case of junior high school teaching 76.3 per cent offer a four-year course. However, four years of training are not required for certification except in two states. In fact, the certification requirements in the different states are so varied that it may be concluded that large numbers of teachers are certified to teach in both junior and senior high schools without having had four years of training. The tendency to increase the course to four years points to an increased amount of academic preparation for high school teaching. (See Table IV.)

The facts revealed by Tables III and IV indicate that the student-teaching course may be taken long before the end of the student's preparation for the profession of secondary teaching. Assuming that a greater amount of preparation is desirable before the student enters into teaching, it is possible to increase the amount of training prior to the student-teaching course.

TABLE IV

NUMBER OF YEARS DEVOTED BY THE DIFFERENT INSTITUTIONS TO THE TRAINING OF JUNIOR AND SENIOR HIGH SCHOOL TEACHERS

	TWO YEARS	THREE YEARS	FOUR YEARS
Junior high course	6	7	42
Senior high course	1	2	51

Number of institutions considered 55

College Year in Which the Student-Teaching Course Is Given. Another approach to the problem of academic preparation that the student-teacher has had prior to taking the course in student-teaching is made in determining in what college year the course is taken. The responses to the questionnaire indicate that the general practice is to require this course in the junior or senior year. Six of the fifty-five institutions do not specify in what year the course must be taken. (See Table V.)

In preparation for senior high school teaching there is a marked tendency to require the course in the senior year; thirty-one institutions require the course in the senior year while fifteen require it in either the junior or the senior year. Fully one-half of the institutions require the course in junior and senior years in preparation for junior high school teaching; the other institutions provide that it may be taken in the sophomore year. In no case may the student-teaching course be taken in the freshman year.

College Credit Given for the Student-Teaching Course. Wide range of practices is noted in the amount of college credit that is

TABLE V

YEAR IN WHICH THE STUDENT TAKES THE COURSE IN PREPARATION FOR
JUNIOR AND SENIOR HIGH SCHOOL SERVICE

	JUNIOR HIGH SCHOOL	SENIOR HIGH SCHOOL
Freshman	0	0
Sophomore	4	0
Junior	5	2
Senior	18	31
Sophomore or junior	1	0
Sophomore or senior	1	0
Junior or senior	11	15
Sophomore, junior, or senior	15	1
No requirement	6	6

Number of institutions considered 55

given for the course in student-teaching. Through the questionnaire
to the directors of training, data were secured from fifty institutions with regard to this item. Ten institutions require two to four
semester-hours as a minimum; one gives a maximum of twenty-
five semester-hours' credit for the course. The most common
practice is to give eight semester-hours' credit for the course.

Adequacy of student-teaching facilities is one of the determining factors in the amount of credit given for the course. If
facilities are plentiful or unlimited there is a tendency to give more
credit; in those cases in which facilities are lacking, there is a
tendency to reduce the credit given.

TABLE VI

COLLEGE CREDIT GIVEN FOR STUDENT-TEACHING

MINIMUM SEMESTER-HOURS	NUMBER OF INSTITUTIONS	MAXIMUM SEMESTER-HOURS	NUMBER OF INSTITUTIONS
2– 4	10	2– 4	5
5– 7	9	5– 7	6
8–10	14	8–10	13
11–13	6	11–13	4
14–16	9	14–16	11
17–19	1	17–19	3
20–22	1	20–22	1
23–25	0	23–25	1

Number of institutions considered 50

NATURE OF STUDENT-TEACHING ACTIVITIES IN SUBJECT-MATTER
COURSES

Observation of the classwork in the laboratory schools is the only type of student-teaching activity carried on in connection with the courses in subject-matter. Of the fifty-four institutions reporting on this matter in reply to the questionnaire sent to the directors of training, thirty-nine report that observation in connection with subject-matter courses is followed as a practice, although the amount of such observation is not known by the directors of training.

The instructors in subject-matter courses prepare the students for the observation work by providing direction sheets and, in some cases, manuals of observation. In practically all cases definite instructions are given to the students prior to the observations made. Most of the institutions require the students to write up the results of the observations made. (See Table VII.)

TABLE VII

NATURE OF STUDENT-TEACHING ACTIVITIES IN SUBJECT-MATTER COURSES

TYPE	YES	No
Students observe classwork for specific techniques and procedures	39	15
Careful preparation is made by class before going in to observe	35	18
Students write up the results of their observations	34	20
Students are furnished direction sheets, manuals for observation	30	20
Number of institutions considered 54		

NATURE OF STUDENT-TEACHING ACTIVITIES IN PROFESSIONAL
COURSES

The directors of training state that the student-teaching activities carried on in connection with education courses are largely of the observation type. Some of the activities, however, closely resemble participation inasmuch as the students assist in the work of giving educational tests and measurements, coach plays, and keep records for classes and rooms. No case was reported, however, in which the student-teacher took complete charge of the classwork.

Of the fifty institutions reporting on this item in the questionnaire, forty-four indicate that observations are carried on in connection with education courses. In approximately three-fourths
of the institutions students are furnished direction sheets for ob-
serving, and write up their findings.

The number of observations carried on in connection with education courses is not known by the directors of training. Observation of classwork is a common practice among the teachers
colleges, judging from the number reporting in the affirmative,
although there does not appear to be a clearly defined policy in
regard to the amount of observation, and the method of doing it.

TABLE VIII

NATURE OF STUDENT-TEACHING ACTIVITIES IN PROFESSIONAL COURSES

ACTIVITY	YES	No
Students observe classwork for specific techniques and procedures	44	6
Students write up their findings	39	11
Assist or give educational tests and measurements	34	15
Coach plays	27	23
Students furnished directions for observing	36	13
Help to keep records of class and room	25	24

Number of institutions considered 50

COÖPERATION AMONG FACULTY MEMBERS IN THE WORK OF THE
STUDENT-TEACHING COURSE

What responsibilities are assumed by the various faculty members other than those directly responsible for the work of the
student-teaching course? The purpose in this discussion is to determine the extent to which coöperation exists. If it is found
that the organization of the institution is such that all staff members have some responsibility in connection with the student-teaching course, we may conclude that a serious attempt is being made
to integrate the entire training program, both subject-matter and
education. This question has bearing on the professionalization
of the entire program. It also reveals something of the attitude
of those who formulate the general institutional policies as well as
of the instructors themselves.

Three questions are raised in this connection, namely: Who assign the students to their student-teaching activities? After assignment, who are responsible for guiding the students? Who determine the student-teacher's mark for the course? The answers to these questions reveal whether the work of the course is an institutional affair, in which all instructors have some part in the training of the student, or whether the responsibility is placed on a group set aside for that purpose.

The questionnaire answers indicate that in general the directors of training are responsible for assigning the student-teachers to their work. The training-teachers and supervisors in the department often assist in this responsibility, however. In five institutions of the fifty-five reporting on this study, subject-matter instructors have responsibility in the assignment of student-teachers. In only two institutions were subject-matter heads completely responsible for the assignment of student-teachers. (See Table IX.)

TABLE IX

INDIVIDUALS RESPONSIBLE FOR ASSIGNING STUDENTS TO STUDENT-TEACHING
ACTIVITIES

	No.
1. Director of Training	31
2. Director and Critic-Teacher	9
3. Director and Subject-Matter Head	2
4. Director of Training and Director of Secondary Education	2
5. Principal of Training School and Critic	2
6. Director of Training, President, Critic	1
7. Director of Training, Head of Subject-Matter Department, Critic	1
8. Director of Training, Dean, Critic	1
9. Critic-Teacher	3
10. Head of Subject-Matter Department	2

Those Responsible for Student-Teacher's Work After Assignment Has Been Made. In reply to the question, "Who are responsible for the student-teacher's work after he has been assigned?" the directors of training state that this work is done largely by a staff specifically set aside for this purpose. In ten institutions out of the fifty-five responding to the questionnaire, subject-matter instructors have responsibility in connection with the student-teacher's work after his assignment, and this responsibility is shared with the director of training and the training-teachers. In two cases the director of training has complete responsibility, whereas in sixteen cases the training-teachers have full responsibility. In twenty-seven cases the responsibility is shared by the director of training, critic-teachers, and the high school principal in charge of the student-teaching center.

TABLE X

THOSE RESPONSIBLE FOR STUDENT-TEACHER'S WORK AFTER HIS
ASSIGNMENT TO STUDENT-TEACHING

	No.
Director of Training and Critic	24
Critic or Training-Teacher alone	16
Director of Training, Head of Subject-Matter Department, Critic	10
Director of Practice	2
Director of Training, Principal of High School, and Critic	3
Number of institutions considered	55

From the above data it is clear that the responsibility for this work is largely a departmental matter; this work is delegated to the department of student-teaching. These data show a lack of integration of the various forces that contribute to the training of the student-teacher.

Student-Teacher's Mark for Course in Student-Teaching. The student-teacher's mark for the course is determined by the training-teachers in forty-six out of fifty-five institutions; the director of student-teaching shares this responsibility in twenty-nine institutions out of the fifty-five reporting in this study. In only eight institutions was there coöperation between various staff members in determining a mark for the course.

TABLE XI

DETERMINATION OF STUDENT-TEACHER'S MARK FOR COURSE IN
STUDENT-TEACHING

	No.
By Training-Teacher	46
By Director or Supervisor of Student-Teaching	29
By Principal of School	9
All have part	8
Number of institutions considered	55

These data again reveal the fact that student-teaching is conceived as the responsibility of a special department and they show lack of coördination of the work among the different staff members. Since the work of the course is left to one department, it is clear that the content is determined by the group having complete responsibility in the matter; and that after the student enters upon responsible teaching, the responsibility of developing his classroom skill and technique is not shared by those members of the faculty who teach education and subject-matter courses.

SUMMARY

The following summary, based upon the data submitted above, may be considered an answer to the first question of the study, "How are the teachers colleges organized to give professional training to prospective secondary teachers?"

1. In 56.7 per cent of the institutions reporting, the program of student-teaching is directed by one individual, usually designated as the "director of training." In 20 per cent of the institutions the work is included within the department of education, in which case the title "head, department of education, and director of student-teaching" is given. In two institutions, this person has the title of "director of practice"; in five others he has the title of "supervisor of practice." In six institutions the director coöperates with others in taking care of the responsibilities of the work.

2. The typical director of training possesses the A.M. degree. One-third of the directors possess the doctor's degree. Only one had less than a master's degree.

3. All the training teachers coöperating possess the A.B. degree. One-third possess the A.M. degree, and about ten per cent have done work toward the doctorate.

4. The median case indicated that the laboratory facilities are in the ratio of two pupils to one college senior student enrolled. In those institutions which provide off-campus facilities the ratio of pupils to college senior enrollment is proportionately larger. The range in the provision for laboratory facilities was great; the lowest being 0.2 pupils to one college senior student enrolled, the highest being 68.7 pupils to one college senior student enrolled. Five institutions indicated that their facilities are unlimited.

5. The typical training-teacher is assigned four student-teachers

at one time in addition to a full-time teaching load. There is a wide variation of practices in the number assigned at one given time, the range being from one to thirty.

6. These data reveal that there is a great diversity of practice in the amount of work required of the student in the major and minor subjects before assignment to student-teaching. The student, in the typical situation, teaches his major subject after having had approximately two years of college preparation or sixteen semester-hours in that subject, and one year of college preparation or eight semester-hours in his minor subject.

7. There is a decided trend toward the four-year course in the training of secondary teachers. However, certification requirements in many of the states make it possible for students to be certified to teach at almost any level beyond the freshman year.

8. Students are usually assigned to their student-teaching during the junior and senior years of their training. In the case of those students training for senior high school service, the tendency is to assign them to their student-teaching in their senior year; students, if preparing for junior high school service, are often trained in the junior year. A few institutions assign students to their training in their sophomore year.

9. College credit for student-teaching ranges from two semester-hours to twenty-five semester-hours. The median credit given for student-teaching in the fifty-five teachers colleges considered is eight to ten semester-hours.

10. Observation activities are carried on in connection with subject-matter courses to a limited degree. The data reveal that observation and participation activities are carried on in education courses, but the extent of such activities is not known by the directors of training.

11. There is little coöperation among faculty members in conducting the work of student-teaching. The work is left, generally, to the director of training and the training-teacher. In only 18.1 per cent of the cases subject-matter heads have limited responsibility in the supervision of student-teaching.

B. THE ORGANIZATION OF THE COURSE ITSELF

INTRODUCTORY STATEMENT

In considering the organization of the course itself, the major activities were determined, and an analysis was made of the amount of time that is allotted to each type of activity. There was agreement among the directors of training, as reported in the questionnaire study, that the following groups of general activities form the content of the course in student-teaching: observation, participation, teaching, conferences, preparation, extra-class, and management and routine.

There is little agreement of practice in the various institutions in the amount of time that is given to the course as a whole and to the separate general activities of the course. The activities occupying the greatest amount of time in the course are: teaching, preparation, observation, and conferences. Participation and extra-class activities occupy a relatively small per cent of the time. Although activities of a management and routine nature occupy an important place in the course, it was impossible to determine how much time is given to these items, since they are usually carried on incidentally and as the need and demand arise. Catalogue descriptions of the courses mention the problems of management and routine as an important phase of the work, and syllabi of the courses in student-teaching invariably stress this phase of the work.

AMOUNT OF TIME GIVEN TO EACH TYPE OF ACTIVITY

The amount of time given to each general activity does not necessarily imply relative importance, but it does indicate the emphasis that is given in the course to the various activities. Consistent with the purpose of the course, teaching activities occupy the greatest amount of time.

Considering the course as a whole, the median number of hours given is 175, with a range of 36 to 630, Q_1 being 110, Q_3 being 318. As stated under the discussions of college credit given for the course and the facilities available for student-teaching in the preceding division of this chapter, the amount of time devoted to the activities of the course is conditioned by the facilities available and the amount of credit given. In those cases in which little college credit is given, it usually follows that less time is given to the course.

In considering the general activities separately, it was found that teaching activities occupied approximately 40 per cent of the time, preparation occupied approximately 30 per cent of the time, while the remaining 30 per cent was divided between participation activities, conferences, and extra-class activities. (Tables XII and XIII.)

TABLE XII

<small>TIME ALLOTMENTS GIVEN TO EACH OF THE ACTIVITIES IN THE COURSE IN STUDENT-TEACHING</small>

GENERAL ACTIVITIES	MEDIAN NUMBER OF HOURS	RANGE	Q₁	Q₃
Observation	25	6–157	12	60
Participation	15	5– 60	10	30
Preparation	60	9–360	36	120
Teaching	72	25–240	60	108
Extra-class activities	11	1– 36	15	18
Conferences	24	5.4– 90	13	40

TABLE XIII

<small>PERCENTAGES OF TIME GIVEN TO DIFFERENT ACTIVITIES IN COURSES IN STUDENT-TEACHING</small>

ACTIVITY	MEDIAN	RANGE	MODE
Observation	15	2.5–50	10
Participation	5	2–30	10
Preparation	28	5–60	35
Teaching	38	10–80	40
Extra-class activities	6	2–17	10
Conferences	8	2–25	10

Number of institutions considered 42

ORGANIZATION OF THE COURSE AS REVEALED BY CATALOGUE DE-
SCRIPTIONS, SYLLABI, AND RATING SCALES

Catalogue Descriptions. An analysis of the descriptions of student-teaching courses in the catalogues of sixty-eight different state teachers colleges that train secondary teachers reveals certain trends regarding the activities emphasized by these institutions. In addition to listing the activities stressed, many describe the general organization and the methods of inducting the student into the activities of the course.

As will be seen from Table XIV, the activities of the nature of responsible teaching are most frequently mentioned. The specific item, teaching under expert supervision, is mentioned most frequently in the descriptions. Activities under the classification of preparation are mentioned next in order of frequency; observation of teaching, personal and professional relationships, management and routine, participation, and application of psychological principles of teaching are the activities in the order of frequency of mention.

Although catalogue descriptions do not always give complete information regarding a course, it is significant to note that the activities suggested in the catalogue closely approximate the activities as reported by the directors of training in the questionnaire study.

The descriptions indicate that the student-teacher is gradually inducted into the work of the course through observation, this activity being the major approach in getting the work established. In some instances, participation in the activities of the class and of the room precede the actual work of responsible teaching. Many of the descriptions state that a serious attempt is made to duplicate the conditions that prevail in regular public high schools, to the end that students may have experience in conducting classwork under conditions similar to those of the public schools. This statement is made in cases where campus schools are used for student-teaching purposes; obviously, the conditions in off-campus schools would be similar to the actual school conditions the student will eventually meet as a high school teacher.

The following catalogue descriptions of the course in student-teaching are typical of those examined:

Education 230—*Supervised Teaching and Management.* Students in this course are assigned to work under the direction of the Training School Supervisors. They have experience in organization of materials for teaching and in all classroom activities, including recreation, supervision of study, and management. Supervised teaching is done under real public school conditions.—State Teachers College, Harrisonburg, Virginia, Bulletin of Information, 1930-31.

Education 327—*Student-Teaching in Secondary Education.* The student is placed in charge of a class under the direction of a critic and supervisor. The mechanics of classroom work are faced constantly by the student and every opportunity is given to form correct habits of teaching through the daily conduct of a class, the management of children, and the use of the technique required of the teacher in actual classwork. Every effort is made to conduct classwork

TABLE XIV

ACTIVITIES OF COURSE IN STUDENT-TEACHING AS REVEALED BY STUDY OF
COURSE DESCRIPTIONS CONTAINED IN CATALOGUES FROM
SIXTY-EIGHT INSTITUTIONS*

ACTIVITY	FREQUENCY OF MENTION
I. Teaching activities (responsible teaching)	
1. Teaching under expert supervision	54
2. Practice in the use of suitable methods	21
3. Practice skills, controls, and techniques essential to class-room teaching	12
4. Practice in the use of standardized tests	9
5. Practice in developing a desirable class presentation	6
II. Preparation (activities in preparation for teaching)	
1. Preparation of lesson plans	52
2. Critical study of subject-matter to be taught	18
3. Making special reports on classwork	13
4. Developing consciousness of the need of daily preparation	2
III. Management, control, and routine (activities involving classroom organization and control)	
1. Directing the mechanics of classroom management and control	30
2. Dealing with practical classroom problems	11
3. Making out records and reports	8
4. Developing a feeling of confidence in dealing with class-room situations	3
IV. Observation (activities in observing classwork and general school routine)	
1. Observation of classwork	45
V. Participation (assisting with classroom problems, and extra-curricular activities)	
1. Participation in classroom activities	22
2. Participation in the conduct of extra-curricular activities	8
3. Participation in community activities	3
VI. Personal and professional relationships (relations with critics, supervisors, and associates)	
1. Conferences with expert teachers	38
2. Criticism of teaching by those in charge	12
3. Developing professional interests and attitudes	5
VII. Application of psychological principles of teaching	
1. Using psychological principles in teaching	18
2. Adapting materials to individual needs and capacities of students	7
3. Study of students to be taught	5
4. Developing interests in materials	3
5. Study of learning situations	2

* See Appendix B, pages 76-78, for a list of the institutions.

under the same conditions as prevail in actual school work in the field.—East Texas State Teachers College, Commerce, Texas, Annual Announcement, Regular Session, 1928-29.

Education 263—*Supervised Student-Teaching.* It is the purpose of this course (1) to develop by practicing the skills, techniques and controls essential to successful classroom procedure in the upper grades in junior high school; and (2) to acquaint the student-teacher with modern devices and materials for teaching. Topics: at first the student-teacher observes activities of the classroom, studies the children and the subject matter he intends to teach. Under the training-teacher's supervision lessons are planned and help given in performance of routine. At least two different subjects are taught during the term. If a student-teacher has a special subject in which he is taking a major or a minor, he may do one-half of his student-teaching in that subject. All student-teachers meet the training teacher under whom they work for one-hour conference period daily.—Eastern Kentucky State Teachers College, Richmond, Kentucky, Catalogue, 1930-31.

Education 403—*Supervised Teaching.* The work in student-teaching is done in the junior and the senior high schools of the State of New Jersey. Experienced and well-trained teachers in these high schools are chosen for training-teachers or supervisors under whose guidance the student-teachers are trained. For twelve weeks the student devotes his entire time to observation, participation in school and classroom activities, and teaching in the major and minor subjects in which he has been specifically prepared. Sixteen term hours credit are given for this work.

The supervision of the student is accomplished through supervisory help given by the departments of subject matter and integration of the college, and by various staff members of the high school. A large responsibility for supervision is placed in the training-teacher in the high school selected as the training center. The following agencies contribute to the direction of the students' activities during assignment:

(1) the training-teacher
(2) the principal of the high school of the training center
(3) the heads of departments and staff members from the departments of subject matter from the college
(4) heads of departments or supervisors in the system to which the student is assigned   ·
(5) supervisors from the integration department
(6) the Director of Student-Teaching from the college

Education 403—(Continued)

A director of student-teaching serves as a coordinator of the program. In the individual and group conferences which are frequently held, the students' problems are frankly considered, and constructive criticisms are offered for improvement. In the group conferences the students are brought back to the campus for an entire day. This enables them to renew their contacts with college activities and at the same time to secure help and advice from various staff members. Usually two such conferences are held during the twelve weeks' period of student-teaching.—New Jersey State Teachers College at Montclair, Catalogue, 1931-32.

The work in the Training Department consists of teaching, observation, making of lesson plans, assisting the training-teacher in various ways, making written reports, attending conferences and general meetings, and becoming familiar with the course of study and workings of the school.—Michigan State Normal College Bulletin, 1929-30, p. 291.

. . . Each student-teacher is required to write out the plans of recitation one week in advance. These plans are closely examined by the training-teachers and, where necessary, discussed with the student-teacher and revised. The instruction itself is also observed by the training-teacher and helpful criticisms are given in private. Each practicing teacher is held fully responsible for the control and management, as well as for the instruction, of the class. He is expected to develop skill and power in management and instruction of a class as a whole and at the same time to study and adapt the work to the individuality and disposition of each pupil.—Bulletin of the Illinois State Normal University, Normal, Illinois, Published April, 1930, p. 118.

The following description of the student-teaching program is taken from the introductory part of the bulletin for 1929-30 of the State Teachers College at Greeley, Colorado.

The Training School, as a laboratory, is a teaching and testing laboratory, rather than a research laboratory. It provides an opportunity for student-teachers who have a sufficient knowledge of subject matter and the theory and principles of education to clarify these and receive practice in the solution of the daily problems and management under the supervision of expert training-teachers. New methods that save time, new schemes for better preparing the children for life, new curricula and courses of study are continually considered by this school and tried out, provided they are sound educationally. . . . Effort is made to maintain such standards of excellence in the work that it may at all times be offered as a demonstration of good teaching under conditions as nearly normal as possible in all respects. . . . The train-ing-teacher is at all times responsible for the entire work of his grade or subject. The Training Schools are planned on the theory that the best interests of student-teachers and the best interests of the ele-mentary and secondary pupils can be made to harmonize. Whatever interferes with the proper development of one interferes with the proper development of the other. . . .

Manuals, Syllabi, and Descriptive Bulletins. A study of man-uals, syllabi, and descriptive bulletins of the courses in student-teaching which prepare secondary teachers indicates that those responsible for the programs are in agreement concerning the major activities of the course. There is lack of agreement, how-ever, with regard to the underlying principles that govern the administration of the different activities. It is apparent that the directors of training and others who have responsibilities in admin-istering the course have objectives in mind that are common to all, but their method of attaining these objectives is different. This lack of agreement in procedure is due to conflicting opinions with regard to the value of certain activities, different forms of or-ganization, and, in some cases, to lack of laboratory facilities.

The printed materials examined showed the same emphasis on a mastery of skills required in classroom teaching as was observed in connection with catalogue descriptions, and as will be pointed out later in connection with the activity analysis of the course. The activities most frequently mentioned under the caption of classroom teaching are: lesson-planning, methods of procedure, principles of learning, routine, and management. Few syllabi mention extra-class activities, community activities, faculty and departmental meetings, etc. as a part of student-teaching courses.

Observation and teaching are invariably mentioned as the activities in which all student-teachers engage. The conference, individual and group, always supplements the work of the course. There are few exceptions in the requirement of detailed lesson plans, and no exceptions in the case of conferences. In a few cases, special demonstration lessons are planned in connection with the work of the course.

Rating Scales. Some form of rating scale is used by most of the teachers colleges in their student-teaching courses. Fifty-two of the fifty-five institutions considered in this study, or 94.6 per cent, use a rating scale. Although there are practically as many forms of scales as there are institutions, it is of interest to note that the larger headings on the scales usually agree. The specific items under these headings vary according to the particular point of view of those who are in charge of the programs of teacher-training.

An examination of a limited number (twenty) of the rating cards used by the institutions coöperating in this study reveals the activities which are given the greatest emphasis. Since rating scales are used to determine the student-teacher's growth and to set up the major activities in which the student-teacher must engage, it follows that such scales should reveal the content of the course as conceived by those responsible for the work.

This study is concerned with the activities as they appear on the rating scales. The form and use of rating scales have been discussed by others, particularly Mead.[4] An analysis of the rating scales examined reveals the fact that the major headings may be grouped under the following:

1. *Personality Factors*
The social, mental, and physical characteristics of the student-teacher are listed under this heading.

2. *Equipment*
Under this heading appear such items as: "knowledge of subject-matter," "background in the subject-matter of related fields," "breadth of information," "understanding of the aims and objectives of the school," "professonal interest," "understanding of students," etc.

3. *Teaching Processes*
The techniques, methods, and procedures followed by the student-teacher in the course in student-teaching are listed. Psychological principles of learning and teaching are included under this heading.

4. *Management*
In this division appear such items as "disciplinary control," "morale of the group," "economy of time," "order," "system," and other items that relate to the problem of setting up desirable teaching situations.

5. *Routine*
Records, reports, supplies, the care and use of supplementary materials, and the ability to use the physical equipment properly, are listed under this heading.

[4] Mead, A. R., *Supervised Student-Teaching*, pp. 467-512. Johnson Publishing Company, 1931.

6. *Growth*

In many of the rating scales, the student-teacher's personal and professional growth are considered. "Growth in teaching power" often appears. Relatively few evaluate the student-teacher's efficiency by determining the "pupil's growth" while under his instruction.

CONFERENCES—INDIVIDUAL AND GROUP

The individual and group conference, conducted in connection with the course in student-teaching, by all of the teachers colleges, is considered of great importance by those directors of training who in the questionnaire study reported the purposes of the conference held in connection with the course. Some directors state that this activity, if properly conducted, is the most fruitful experience the student has during the progress of the course. The student's efforts to carry out the work of teaching are analyzed and evaluated, and attempts are made to correct wrong procedures and to strengthen and develop those skills and abilities which have been initiated.

It is difficult to determine the exact content of the conferences held in connection with the student-teaching courses. The directors of training were asked, in the questionnaire, to state the three major purposes of conferences. Forty-four directors listed twenty-nine different purposes. "Discussion of the specific aims of the lesson to be taught" is listed by approximately one-third of the directors of training as an important purpose. Other purposes of major importance are: "discussion of lesson plans," "development of personality qualities," "criticism of the student's selection of subject-matter," and "development of an interest in professional growth."

If the twenty-nine different purposes are analyzed it will be found that they may be grouped under three major headings, in the following order of frequency of mention: *first*, purposes relating to the student's use of the fundamental techniques of teaching; *second*, purposes relating to the student's personal and professional growth; and *third*, purposes relating to the selection and organization of subject-matter. (See Table XV.)

SUMMARY

This summary may be considered an answer to the question, "How are the courses in student-teaching organized and administered to carry out the program of training which the institutions

TABLE XV

PURPOSES OF THE CONFERENCE AS STATED BY DIRECTORS OF TRAINING

	FREQUENCY OF MENTION
1. Discussion of the specific aims of the lesson to be taught ...	16
2. Discussion of lesson plans	15
3. Development of personality qualities	13
4. Criticism of student's selection of subject-matter	12
5. Developing an interest in professional growth	12
6. Build up correct standards of teaching	11
7. To review observations made, and check	11
8. To outline acceptable techniques	10
9. Criticism of the student's organization of subject-matter ...	9
10. Helping student solve his own problems	7
11. Directing the student in self-criticism	7
12. Criticism of the student's presentation of subject-matter ...	7
13. To diagnose pupil's needs and difficulties	6
14. Supervisors give the student constructive aid in understanding children	5
15. To develop the student's perspective	4
16. Discussion of the specific problems of the class	4
17. Developing good morale—good will, right attitudes, spirit of cooperation	4
18. Decision is made in conferences on what the strong and weak points are	4
19. Teaching students to apply principles which he already knows	3
20. Show importance of definite assignments	2
21. Show how to improve management	2
22. To aid in the recognition of ethical relationships	2
23. To help the student to get ready for his future activities ...	2
24. For orientation purposes—if too timid, encourage; if too cocksure, show shortcomings	2
25. Humanizing the experience	2
26. Anticipate the difficulties student is likely to meet	1
27. Discuss problem cases	1
28. Conference helps the training-teacher to better understand the student's personal background	1
29. To find out if the student knows the subject-matter to be taught	1

Number of directors of training responding 44

have set up?" These data were secured by means of a questionnaire sent to the directors of training, and by a study of catalogue descriptions, syllabi of the course in student-teaching, and rating cards used by the various training departments.

1. There is agreement that the types of activities in the course fall under the following captions, namely: observation, participa-

tion, preparation, teaching, extra-class activities, and conferences.

2. There is no agreement as to the amount of time that should be allotted to the different types of activities. In the case of observation the range of time spent on this activity is from 2.5 per cent to 50.0 per cent of the total time given to all the activities of the course in student-teaching. In teaching activities, the range is from 10 per cent to 80 per cent of the total time spent on all the activities of the course.

3. There is a tendency showing that if laboratory facilities are plentiful the student-teacher engages in more hours of teaching, whereas if laboratory facilities are lacking there is an increase in the time given to the activities other than teaching.

4. A study of catalogue descriptions of the course reveals a tendency toward a mastery of classroom techniques.

5. A study of manuals, syllabi, descriptive bulletins, and rating scales shows that the chief purpose of the course is to secure a mastery of classroom technique with further emphasis on the development of personality traits.

6. The conference is a part of all student-teaching programs in the institutions considered. The major emphasis in the conferences is given to the following types of activities: discussion of the techniques of teaching, criticism of the student's work in executing the activities of the course, improvement of personality traits, and developing a professional point of view.

CHAPTER III

THE CONTENT OF THE COURSE AS REVEALED BY AN ACTIVITY ANALYSIS

THE DEVELOPMENT OF AN ACTIVITY LIST

In the preceding chapter it was observed that the major activities of the course in student-teaching are: observation, participation, teaching, extra-class, management and routine, conferences, and preparation. This determination of the larger activities has definite bearing on the organization of the course but it does not give information regarding the nature and content of the specific activities that are included in the course. With the thought of determining these specific activities, a job analysis technique was used. Then the task became one of listing the activities included in the course.

In the preparation of the original list of activities an attempt was made to list all types of activities which have some direct or indirect relationship to the work of teaching. This procedure seemed most desirable since student-teaching courses have been organized with the idea of duplicating actual teaching situations. Following this procedure, the work of selecting activities began. Manuals, syllabi of courses in student-teaching, rating cards, descriptive bulletins, and catalogues were consulted as sources; directors of training, training-teachers, and staff members engaged in the work of teacher-training were asked informally to supplement the list. A group of eighty graduate students whose major interest was in the field of teacher-training suggested additional activities. As a result of this procedure, a list of six hundred activities was evolved.

Upon examination, it was found that there was considerable overlapping in many of the items. Some method of refining the list of activities thus evolved was necessary; many of the activities originally selected should of necessity be eliminated. Since these items had been listed without regard to organization, it seemed desirable to organize them around larger units. This procedure helped in discovering duplications as well as in developing a more logical organization of the materials. Four major headings appeared as a result of this organization, namely: (1) *activities involving classroom instruction,* (2) *activities involving classroom management and control,* (3) *the student's participation in extra-class and community activities,* (4) *and the student-teacher's growth.*

Such an organization takes into account the student-teacher's participation in the work of the classroom, with particular emphasis on the techniques and methods of classroom work. It also takes into account the activities involving the management and routine of the school. A study of the student's participation in extra-class and community activities would include those largely outside the classroom but closely related to the interests of the school and community. The last general topic includes those activities which involve personal and professional growth.

THE DEVELOPMENT OF A MASTER LIST OF ACTIVITIES FOR FINAL EVALUATION

The next problem was one of selecting from the original list compiled the activities which would be later submitted to a jury of experts for final amplification and evaluation. The most scientific list available was that compiled by Charters and Waples in the Commonwealth Teacher-Training Study.[1] This list was consulted for the purpose of verification as well as to aid in the elimination of some activities which have a remote relation to teaching. The Commonwealth Study was of particular value in evolving a list of activities relating to the problem of teaching pupils how to study, and many of the activities suggested by this work under the heading of "How to Study" were incorporated.

Since there have been established no definite scientific criteria in selecting activities for courses in student-teaching, it seemed desirable to set up criteria arbitrarily. The following were used as bases in evolving the master list:

1. Select only those activities which are clearly distinct.
2. Eliminate those which may be included under some other head.
3. Select only those activities which relate directly to the profession of teaching.
4. Eliminate those which are remotely related.

[1] Charters, W. W., and Waples, Douglas, *The Commonwealth Teacher-Training Study,* pp. 564 ff.

With these arbitrary criteria as bases, a master list of one hundred and two activities was compiled. Two juries, the directors of training in state teachers colleges and a sampling of training-teachers in similar institutions, were asked to supplement the list with other activities which, in their judgment, seemed significant. Fifty-five directors of training and one hundred training-teachers representing sixty-nine different state teachers colleges responded with twenty-three additional activities.

The master list of activities thus evolved does not become an exhaustive one, but it may be claimed that it includes the major activities of the course in student-teaching as it is now organized.

MASTER LIST OF ACTIVITIES INCLUDED IN THE COURSE

I. Activities Involving Class Instruction
  A. Planning subject-matter
  1. Selection of materials to be planned
  2. Determining objectives of materials
  3. Organizing subject-matter
  4. Planning methods of presentation
  5. Planning assignments
  6. Planning pupil participation
  7. Determining method for evaluation of pupil's needs, abilities, interests
  8. Planning methods of evaluation of pupil's achievements
  9. The writing of the plan
  10. The use of the plan after its preparation
  11. *The comparison of the plan with others previously used*
  12. *Written record of work after rating the success or failure of the plan in use. Suggestions for improvement for future use*
  13. *Planning of big unit first—then smaller groupings. Use of plan as retrospective aid*

  B. The selection and organization of subject-matter for instruction
  1. Determining the general objectives for grade and subject
  2. Determining specific objectives in harmony with the general objectives
  3. Utilizing objectives selected in teaching subject matter
  4. Mastery of subject-matter taught
  5. Assignments adapted and organized to meet the requirements of the course
  6. Selecting proper materials for study
  7. Consideration of sequence of materials to be taught
  8. *Classification of materials*
  9. *Filing of materials*

  C. Recognition of pupil's interests, abilities, and needs in class instruction
  1. Determining pupil's interests
  2. Using methods of instruction to develop interest

NOTE: Italicized items indicate that the activities were suggested by the directors of training and the training-teachers.

    3. Selecting subject-matter with reference to pupil's abilities
    4. Taking into account pupil's abilities in class instruction
    5. Recognition of individual differences in making assignments
    6. Allowing pupils to assume responsibility in class
    7. Selecting subject-matter with reference to pupil's need

D. Some essential factors in class instruction
    1. Subject-matter selected on basis of needs of class
    2. Methods of presentation suitable to subject-matter
    3. Using drill exercises and problems to fix responses
    4. Using devices for overcoming difficulties
    5. Forming conclusions, summaries
    6. Proper balance of pupil-teacher participation in class instruction
    7. Economical use of time
    8. *Provision for individual differences*

E. Evaluating pupil's achievement
    1. Setting up standards to achieve
    2. Selecting standardized tests
    3. Preparing tests
    4. Administering tests
    5. Diagnosing pupil's difficulties and needs
    6. Follow-up of diagnosis made
    7. Evaluating test papers
    8. *Helping pupils to evaluate their own work*
    9. *Achievement in terms of attitudes formed*

F. General activities in teaching pupils how to study
    1. Teaching pupils to develop useful interests, worthy motives, and sincere appreciations
    2. Teaching pupils to develop traits and habits
    3. Teaching pupils to develop individual tendencies and abilities
    4. Teaching pupils to solve problems
    5. Teaching pupils how to improve skills and abilities
    6. Teaching pupils to make practical use of materials studied
    7. Teaching pupils to make economical use of time

G. Specific techniques in teaching pupils how to study
    1. Teaching pupils to decide what is to be done
    2. Teaching pupils to foresee results to be obtained
    3. Teaching pupils to plan methods of work
    4. Teaching pupils to gather reading materials
    5. Teaching pupils to find desired information from reading material
    6. Teaching pupils to obtain a proper perspective of the course
    7. Teaching pupils to maintain a critical attitude toward material studied
    8. Teaching pupils to prepare for classwork
    9. Teaching pupils to locate specific problems
    10. Teaching pupils to analyze problems
    11. Teaching pupils to organize material in proper form
    12. Teaching pupils to summarize material
    13. Teaching pupils to combine ideas in proper relationships
    14. Teaching pupils to discuss implications of material studied
    15. Teaching pupils to find or make illustrations for greater clearness
    16. Teaching pupils to note, outline, and record useful information

17. Teaching pupils to take tests and examinations efficiently
18. Teaching pupils to compare work with standards in order to check errors
19. Teaching pupils to correct errors
20. *Teaching pupils to concentrate*
21. *Teaching pupils to have a specific place to study*

II. Activities Involving Classroom Management and Control
  A. Routine factors
    1. Recording attendance
    2. Filling out forms required by the school office
    3. Searching for records of individuals
    4. Searching for records of class groups
    5. Reporting achievement of classwork
    6. Maintaining proper temperature in classroom
    7. Securing proper lighting of classroom
    8. Care of the ventilation of the classroom
    9. Making classroom attractive
    10. Making available the supplies for teaching
    11. *Use of charts and other materials in discipline*
    12. *Making permanent class records, and individual records*
    13. *Making classroom free from distractions*
  B. Activities involving pupil and student-teacher relationships
    1. Teaching pupils desirable attitudes and ideals
    2. Teaching the school's regulations
    3. Rewarding meritorious conduct
    4. Penalizing misdemeanors
    5. Applying preventive measures in directing children
    6. Respect for the desires and welfare of pupils
    7. Teaching pupils to work independently
    8. Establishing cordial relationships with pupils
    9. *Teaching to work coöperatively*

III. The Student-Teacher's Part in Extra-Class and Community Activities
  A. Extra-class activities
    1. Assists in planning and directing assembly programs
    2. Participates in school campaigns and drives
    3. Directs club activities
    4. Chaperons groups
    5. Takes pupils on excursions
    6. Acts as official judge in contests
    7. Coaches pupils
    8. *Playground supervision*
    9. *Lunchroom duties*
    10. Acts as adviser to pupil's own organizations

  B. Community activities
    1. Gives advice and information to parents
    2. Meets socially with parents—teachers
    3. Participates in parent-teacher meetings
    4. Visits commercial and service clubs and organizations of community
    5. Establishes contacts with church interests
    6. Assists in community drives and campaigns

IV. The Student-Teacher's Growth
   A. Personal factors
      1. Analysis of personality traits in others
      2. Self-analysis of personality
      3. Methods devised to improve traits
      4. *Appearance*
   B. Professional factors
      1. Develop interest in teaching as a profession
      2. Reading of professional periodicals
      3. Information given about the best professional organizations
      4. Teaching means of "growth in service"
      5. *Ethics of profession*
      6. *Cultural growth*
      7. *Professional attitude*
      8. *Resourcefulness*

SUMMARY

The question, "In what activities does the student-teacher engage while pursuing the course in student-teaching?" is answered in this chapter.

1. From a list of six hundred activities selected at random and without regard to organization a master list of one hundred and two activities was made. After considering all the activities as to type, the following main headings were determined, namely: activities involving classroom instruction, activities involving classroom management and control, the student's participation in extra-class and community activities, and the student-teacher's growth.

2. One hundred and two activities were submitted to the directors of training and the training-teachers. These officials were requested to check the list for completeness and to add such activities as, in their judgment, should be added in order to make a complete list. Twenty-three such activities were suggested by the one hundred and fifty-five individuals coöperating. Some of those suggested are vital and valuable. In some cases, however, there is a repetition of activities in the master list.

3. In view of the representative groups that checked the list and of the opinions given by the two juries of workers engaged in the course in student-teaching, it is believed that the list, although not exhaustive, represents the most important activities of the course in student-teaching.

CHAPTER IV

THE ACTIVITIES INCLUDED IN THE COURSE IN STUDENT-TEACHING AND THE RELATIVE IMPORTANCE OF EACH ACTIVITY

INTRODUCTION

In the preceding chapter an attempt was made to determine the activities that are of major importance in the student-teaching course. With this objective in mind a master list of one hundred and two activities was evolved, and further supplemented by twenty-three activities suggested by the directors of training and training-teachers. Although not an exhaustive list, it is believed that the activities selected are basic in the courses in student-teaching designed for training secondary teachers.

Several questions are pertinent in a consideration of the activity list as developed and described in the previous chapter. Which activities are included in the courses in student-teaching? Of what relative importance is each activity? In what courses of the curriculum are these activities taught? Answers to these questions not only will give the content of the course as it is now organized, but will also locate the activity with regard to its relative importance.

The directors of training considered the activity list in relation to their courses and checked those items which they include in their courses. This same group also gave information concerning the placement of the activity in the courses of the curriculum of the teachers colleges. Two groups, the directors of training and the training-teachers, checked the list of activities, giving their judgments as to the relative importance of each of the items in the master list.

Another factor of importance is a determination as to where the activities should be taught. If the content of these activities is introduced or taught in connection with the subject-matter and education courses, the tendency to professionalize the work of these courses is clearly the policy. The data secured reveal the attitude or point of view which is held by the various institutions toward the policy of professionalizing subject-matter materials.

THE ACTIVITIES INCLUDED IN THE COURSE IN STUDENT-TEACHING

The directors of training in forty-six institutions checked the master list, indicating, in each case, whether or not the activity is taught in the course in student-teaching which they offer. Only the one hundred and two activities submitted for checking are considered in this study; the twenty-three additional activities suggested by the directors of training and the training-teachers are not included.

The percentage of schools including each activity in its course in student-teaching is indicated in Table XVI.

TABLE XVI

THE ACTIVITIES INCLUDED IN THE STUDENT-TEACHING COURSE

ACTIVITY	Percentage of State Teachers Colleges which Include the Activity in Their Course in Student Teaching
I. Activities involving class instruction	
A. Planning subject-matter	
1. Selection of materials to be planned	91.3
2. Determining objectives of materials	80.4
3. Organizing subject-matter	89.1
4. Planning methods of presentation	89.1
5. Planning assignments	89.1
6. Planning pupil participation	86.9
7. Determining method for evaluation of pupil's needs, abilities, interests	82.5
8. Planning methods of evaluation of pupil's achievements	89.1
9. The writing of the plan	89.1
10. The use of the plan after its preparation	95.6
B. The selection and organization of subject-matter for instruction	
1. Determining the general objectives for grade and subject	62.1
2. Determining specific objectives in harmony with the general objectives	76.1
3. Utilizing objectives selected in teaching subject-matter	93.4
4. Mastery of subject-matter taught	73.9
5. Assignments adapted and organized to meet the requirements of the course	84.7

TABLE XVI (*Continued*)

THE ACTIVITIES INCLUDED IN THE STUDENT-TEACHING COURSE (*Continued*)

ACTIVITY	Percentage of State Teachers Colleges which Include the Activity in Their Course in Student Teaching
6. Selecting proper materials for study	84.7
7. Consideration of sequence of materials to be taught	82.5
C. Recognition of pupil's interests, abilities, and needs in class instruction	
1. Determining pupil's interests	87.0
2. Using methods of instruction to develop interest ...	82.5
3. Selecting subject-matter with reference to pupil's abilities	91.3
4. Taking into account pupil's abilities in class instruction	89.1
5. Recognition of individual differences in making assignments	89.1
6. Allowing pupils to assume responsibility in class ...	93.4
7. Selecting subject-matter with reference to pupil's needs	89.1
D. Some essential factors in class instructing	
1. Subject matter selected on basis of needs of class ..	91.3
2. Methods of presentation suitable to subject-matter	73.9
3. Using drill exercises and problems to fix responses ..	84.7
4. Using devices for overcoming difficulties	80.4
5. Forming conclusions, summaries	82.5
6. Proper balance of pupil-teacher participation in class instruction	78.2
7. Economical use of time	82.5
E. Evaluating pupil's achievement	
1. Setting up standards to achieve	78.2
2. Selecting standardized tests	58.6
3. Preparing tests	78.2
4. Administering tests	91.3
5. Diagnosing pupil's difficulties and needs	89.1
6. Follow-up of diagnosis made	91.3
7. Evaluating test papers	93.4
F. General activities in teaching pupils to study	
1. Teaching pupils to develop useful interests, worthy motives, and sincere appreciations	89.1
2. Teaching pupils to develop traits and habits	87.0
3. Teaching pupils to develop individual tendencies and abilities	80.4
4. Teaching pupils to solve problems	95.6
5. Teaching pupils how to improve skills and abilities .	89.1
6. Teaching pupils to make practical use of materials studied	97.8
7. Teaching pupils to make economical use of time ...	87.0

TABLE XVI (*Continued*)

THE ACTIVITIES INCLUDED IN THE STUDENT-TEACHING COURSE (*Continued*)

ACTIVITY	Percentage of State Teachers Colleges which Include the Activity in Their Course in Student Teaching
G. Specific techniques in teaching pupils how to study	
1. Teaching pupils to decide what is to be done	80.4
2. Teaching pupils to foresee results to be obtained ...	80.4
3. Teaching pupils to plan methods of work	82.5
4. Teaching pupils to gather reading materials	87.0
5. Teaching pupils to find desired information from reading material	87.0
6. Teaching pupils to obtain a proper perspective of the course	87.0
7. Teaching pupils to maintain a critical attitude toward material studies	80.4
8. Teaching pupils to prepare for classwork	91.3
9. Teaching pupils to locate specific problems	82.5
10. Teaching pupils to analyze problems	89.1
11. Teaching pupils to organize material in proper form	91.3
12. Teaching pupils to summarize material	93.4
13. Teaching pupils to combine ideas in proper relationship	82.5
14. Teaching pupils to discuss implications of material studied	89.1
15. Teaching pupils to find or make illustrations for greater clearness	82.5
16. Teaching pupils to note, outline, and record useful information	87.0
17. Teaching pupils to take tests and examinations efficiently	82.5
18. Teaching pupils to compare work with standards in order to check errors	76.1
19. Teaching pupils to correct errors	89.1
II. Activities involving classroom management and control	
A. Routine factors	
1. Recording attendance	91.3
2. Filling out forms required by the school office	91.3
3. Searching for records of individuals	71.7
4. Searching for records of class groups	71.7
5. Reporting achievement of classwork	91.3
6. Maintaining proper temperature in classroom	91.3
7. Securing proper lighting of classroom	91.3
8. Care of the ventilation of the classroom	91.3
9. Making classroom attractive	91.3
10. Making available the supplies for teaching	87.0

TABLE XVI (*Continued*)

THE ACTIVITIES INCLUDED IN THE STUDENT-TEACHING COURSE (*Continued*)

ACTIVITY	Percentage of State Teachers Colleges which Include the Activity in Their Course in Student Teaching
B. Activities involving pupil and student-teacher relationship	
1. Teaching pupils desirable attitudes and ideals	91.3
2. Teaching the school's regulations	95.6
3. Rewarding meritorious conduct	91.3
4. Penalizing misdemeanors	91.3
5. Applying preventive measures in directing children	100.0
6. Respect for the desires and welfare of pupils	100.0
7. Teaching pupils to work independently	100.0
8. Establishing cordial relationships with pupils	100.0
III. The student-teacher's part in extra-class and community activities	
A. Extra-class activities	
1. Assists in planning and directing assembly programs	80.4
2. Participates in school campaigns and drives	60.8
3. Directs club activities	73.9
4. Chaperons groups	73.9
5. Takes pupils on excursions	82.5
6. Acts as official judge in contests	76.1
7. Coaches pupils	82.5
B. Community activities	
1. Gives advice and information to parents	47.8
2. Meets socially with parent-teachers	67.8
3. Participates in parent-teacher meetings	58.6
4. Visits commercial and service clubs and organizations of community	43.4
5. Establishes contact with church interests	34.7
6. Assists in community drives and campaigns	28.2
IV. The student-teacher's growth	
A. Personal factors	
1. Analysis of personality traits in others	63.0
2. Self-analysis of personality	63.0
3. Methods devised to improve traits	63.0
B. Professional factors	
1. Develop interest in teaching as a profession	71.7
2. Reading of professional periodicals	76.1
3. Information given about the best professional organizations	63.0
4. Teaching means of "growth in service"	71.7

For convenience in comparing the activities listed above with those tabulated in the master list of activities (pages 35 to 38), the data of Table XVI are briefly summarized to show the following distribution of activities:

29	activities	are	taught	in	91 to 100%	of the institutions			
38	"	"	"	"	81 to 90%	"	"		"
22	"	"	"	"	71 to 80%	"	"		"
6	"	"	"	"	61 to 70%	"	"		"
3	"	"	"	"	51 to 60%	"	"		"
2	"	"	"	"	41 to 50%	"	"		"
1	"	"	"	"	31 to 40%	"	"		"
1	"	"	"	"	21 to 30%	"	"		"

From the above summary it is seen that the master list of activities, checked by the two groups, includes the activities which make up the course in student-teaching. Ninety per cent of the activities in the master list are taught in the student-teaching courses in three out of every four of the institutions considered in this investigation.

EVALUATIONS PLACED UPON ACTIVITIES BY DIRECTORS OF TRAINING AND TRAINING-TEACHERS

How valuable are the activities in the master list in the courses in student-teaching? Two groups vitally engaged in the work of student-teaching were selected to serve as juries to pass judgment as to the relative value of each activity in the master list. The directors of training and the training-teachers were asked to pass such judgment.

In evaluating each activity, the two groups, the directors of training and the training-teachers, were asked to rank each activity on the scale of 1 to 5, the score 1 representing the degree of greatest importance, the score 5 representing the degree of least importance. Statistical computations of the averages were made to determine the reliability of the judgments of both groups. Then, the correlation of the averages of the two groups, the directors of training and the training-teachers, was determined.

In Table XVII the evaluations made by the two groups are given for each item in the master list. The number of the institutions represented have been translated into percentages in order to be more meaningful to the reader. Finally, the averages of the ratings by each group will be found in the last column. From the averages in this column the statistical computations for reliability and correlation were made.

TABLE XVII

RANK AND AVERAGE OF ACTIVITIES IN THE MASTER LIST AS EVALUATED BY
DIRECTORS OF TRAINING AND TRAINING-TEACHERS

This table should be read as follows: Under the group entitled, "Activities involving Class Instruction," subhead A, item 1, in the activity "selection of materials to be planned," 80.00% of the directors of training (D. of T. in the table) ranked this activity 1; 6.66% ranked it 2; 6.66% ranked it 3; 2.22% ranked it 4; and 4.44% ranked it 5. The average rank of this activity by the directors of training was 1.66.

In considering this same activity, 64.94% of the training teachers (T. T. in the table) ranked this activity 1; etc.

GROUP OF ACTIVITIES	RANK	RANKED PERCENTAGES					AVER-AGE RANK
		1	2	3	4	5	
I. Activities Involving Class Instruction							
A. Planning Subject-Matter							
1. Selection of materials to be planned	D. of T.	80.00	06.66	06.66	02.22	04.44	1.66
	T. T.	64.94	20.61	13.40	01.03	00.00	1.60
2. Determining objectives of materials	D. of T.	57.12	21.42	16.66	02.38	02.38	1.71
	T. T.	62.24	28.57	09.18	00.00	00.00	1.46
3. Organizing subject-matter	D. of T.	67.32	13.95	11.62	04.65	02.32	1.60
	T. T.	61.76	20.58	12.74	03.92	00.98	1.61
4. Planning methods of presentation	D. of T.	65.00	22.50	05.00	02.50	05.00	1.60
	T. T.	54.08	18.36	16.12	09.19	02.04	1.85
5. Planning assignments	D. of T.	55.23	31.96	07.89	02.63	02.63	1.65
	T. T.	51.04	16.66	13.54	14.16	04.16	2.04
6. Planning participation	D. of T.	53.68	26.84	04.88	04.88	09.76	2.00
	T. T.	58.58	17.17	09.09	07.07	08.08	1.88
7. Determining method of evaluation of pupil's needs, abilities, interests	D. of T.	47.80	28.68	09.56	07.17	04.78	2.39
	T. T.	64.28	23.46	08.08	00.00	04.08	1.56
8. Planning methods of evaluation of pupil's achievements	D. of T.	36.82	36.82	07.89	13.15	05.26	2.13
	T. T.	39.78	25.80	15.05	13.97	05.37	2.19
9. The writing of the plan	D. of T.	18.41	23.67	26.30	21.04	07.39	2.69
	T. T.	20.61	19.92	20.61	24.74	14.43	2.96
10. The use of the plan after its preparation	D. of T.	34.19	18.41	26.30	13.15	07.89	2.42
	T. T.	32.95	23.86	26.13	07.95	09.09	2.36
B. The selection and organization of subject-matter for instruction							
1. Determining the general objectives for grade and subject	D. of T.	61.44	15.36	10.24	12.80	00.00	2.36
	T. T.	70.01	20.61	08.24	01.03	00.00	1.40
2. Determining specific objectives in harmony with the general objectives	D. of T.	60.49	13.15	07.89	07.89	10.52	1.94
	T. T.	51.51	31.31	12.12	05.05	00.00	1.70
3. Utilizing objectives selected in teaching subject-matter	D. of T.	60.00	22.50	07.50	07.50	02.50	1.77
	T. T.	48.00	31.00	16.00	03.00	02.00	1.80
4. Mastery of subject-matter taught	D. of T.	87.50	07.50	05.00	00.00	02.50	1.32
	T. T.	79.48	11.22	05.10	03.06	01.02	1.35
5. Assignments adapted and organized to meet the requirements of course	D. of T.	44.32	38.78	08.31	02.77	05.54	1.77
	T. T.	39.17	18.55	21.64	08.24	12.36	2.36
6. Selecting proper materials for study	D. of T.	62.50	32.50	05.00	00.00	00.00	1.42
	T. T.	48.95	29.16	09.37	10.41	02.08	1.87
7. Consideration of sequence of materials to be taught	D. of T.	48.64	23.04	20.48	02.56	05.12	1.92
	T. T.	27.36	36.84	16.84	11.45	07.29	2.34

TABLE XVII (*Continued*)

Group of Activities	Rank	Ranked Percentages					Average Rank
		1	2	3	4	5	
C. Recognition of pupil's interests, abilities, and needs in class instruction							
1. Determining pupil's interest	D. of T.	70.47	19.44	04.86	00.00	14.86	1.48
	T. T.	71.00	21.00	05.00	02.00	01.00	1.41
2. Using methods of instruction to develop interest	D. of T.	59.75	24.30	09.72	02.43	02.43	1.60
	T. T.	61.70	28.72	04.25	04.25	01.06	1.54
3. Selecting subject-matter with reference to pupil's abilities	D. of T.	69.12	17.92	13.80	00.00	00.00	1.43
	T. T.	63.26	25.61	08.08	00.00	03.03	1.55
4. Taking into account pupil's abilities in class instruction	D. of T.	65.61	24.30	07.29	02.43	00.00	1.39
	T. T.	53.60	27.83	11.33	06.18	01.13	1.73
5. Recognition of individual differences in making assignments	D. of T.	58.00	25.52	02.32	06.96	06.96	1.79
	T. T.	50.51	23.71	17.52	06.18	03.09	1.86
6. Allowing pupils to assume responsibility in class	D. of T.	48.64	35.84	05.12	07.68	02.56	1.80
	T. T.	48.42	26.31	12.63	07.36	05.26	1.94
7. Selecting subject-matter with reference to pupil's needs	D. of T.	65.00	27.50	07.50	00.00	00.00	1.35
	T. T.	68.04	19.58	06.18	04.12	03.09	1.55
D. Some essential factors in class instruction							
1. Subject-matter selected on basis of needs of class	D. of T.	68.38	26.30	05.26	00.00	00.00	1.37
	T. T.	77.08	16.66	03.12	02.08	00.00	1.30
2. Methods of presentation suitable to subject-matter	D. of T.	49.97	36.82	13.15	00.00	00.00	1.58
	T. T.	53.60	34.02	11.34	01.03	00.00	1.59
3. Using drill exercises and problems to fix responses	D. of T.	32.40	40.50	13.50	10.80	02.70	1.62
	T. T.	28.12	26.04	25.00	10.41	10.41	2.49
4. Using devices for overcoming difficulties	D. of T.	25.65	49.90	19.95	02.85	11.40	2.34
	T. T.	26.80	27.83	30.92	05.13	09.28	2.42
5. Forming conclusions, summaries	D. of T.	54.00	18.90	24.30	02.70	00.00	1.75
	T. T.	35.48	36.55	17.20	08.60	03.22	2.07
6. Proper balance of pupil-teacher participation in class instruction	D. of T.	49.97	21.04	15.78	07.89	05.26	1.96
	T. T.	54.00	24.00	09.00	10.00	03.00	1.84
7. Economical use of time	D. of T.	56.32	15.36	07.68	05.12	10.24	1.74
	T. T.	51.68	26.96	14.60	03.37	03.37	1.83
E. Evaluating pupil's achievement							
1. Setting up standards to achieve	D. of T.	69.04	14.28	09.50	07.14	00.00	1.52
	T. T.	69.00	26.00	02.00	02.00	01.00	1.40
2. Selecting standardized tests	D. of T.	28.95	23.68	39.47	05.26	05.26	2.42
	T. T.	15.05	37.63	24.73	10.75	11.93	2.64
3. Preparing tests	D. of T.	40.00	32.50	07.50	10.00	10.00	2.17
	T. T.	35.71	29.59	26.53	04.08	04.08	2.10
4. Administering tests	D. of T.	27.02	35.13	16.21	05.40	16.21	2.49
	T. T.	25.51	27.55	18.36	22.44	06.12	2.56
5. Diagnosing pupil's difficulties and needs	D. of T.	83.72	11.62	04.64	00.00	00.00	1.20
	T. T.	79.00	16.00	05.00	00.00	00.00	1.29
6. Follow-up of diagnosis made	D. of T.	68.42	21.05	05.26	05.26	00.00	1.48
	T. T.	67.00	22.00	05.00	04.00	02.00	1.66
7. Evaluating test papers	D. of T.	32.50	32.50	27.50	02.50	05.00	2.15
	T. T.	24.00	30.00	18.00	12.00	16.00	2.66

TABLE XVII (*Continued*)

Group of Activities	Rank	Ranked Percentages					Average Rank
		1	2	3	4	5	
F. General activities in teaching pupils to study							
1. Teaching pupils to develop useful interest, worthy motives, and sincere appreciation	D. of T.	71.43	16.66	04.76	02.38	04.76	1.53
	T. T.	86.00	08.00	03.00	01.00	02.00	1.25
2. Teaching pupils to develop traits and habits	D. of T.	73.81	14.24	07.14	02.38	02.38	1.45
	T. T.	66.31	26.31	05.23	01.05	01.05	1.44
3. Teaching pupils to develop individual tendencies and abilities	D. of T.	46.66	22.22	13.33	08.88	08.88	2.11
	T. T.	50.50	33.33	10.10	03.03	03.03	2.05
4. Teaching pupils to solve problems	D. of T.	74.41	13.95	09.30	00.00	02.32	1.41
	T. T.	61.00	21.00	10.00	03.00	05.00	1.60
5. Teaching pupils how to improve skills and abilities	D. of T.	57.50	22.50	12.50	07.50	02.50	1.72
	T. T.	42.70	31.25	14.58	09.37	02.08	1.96
6. Teaching pupils to make practical use of materials studied	D. of T.	40.49	33.33	07.14	14.28	07.76	2.09
	T. T.	52.59	18.55	15.46	08.24	07.21	2.05
7. Teaching pupils to make economical use of time	D. of T.	61.90	21.43	07.14	07.14	02.38	1.66
	T. T.	54.15	19.79	14.58	06.24	05.20	1.88
G. Specific techniques in teaching pupils how to study							
1. Teaching pupils to decide what is to be done	D. of T.	66.66	33.58	02.56	00.00	00.00	1.35
	T. T.	69.00	26.00	01.00	02.00	02.00	1.42
2. Teaching pupils to foresee results to be obtained	D. of T.	34.09	31.81	11.36	00.00	00.00	1.31
	T. T.	51.57	32.63	06.30	08.40	01.05	1.72
3. Teaching pupils to plan methods of work	D. of T.	52.17	08.69	19.55	02.17	23.92	2.36
	T. T.	60.63	28.72	07.44	03.19	01.06	1.56
4. Teaching pupils to gather reading materials	D. of T.	45.94	35.13	13.51	05.40	00.00	1.78
	T. T.	35.32	39.12	15.21	06.08	04.34	2.06
5. Teaching pupils to find desired information from reading material	D. of T.	50.00	38.88	00.00	05.55	05.55	1.76
	T. T.	52.12	23.40	15.95	07.44	01.06	1.88
6. Teaching pupils to obtain a proper perspective of the course	D. of T.	31.25	31.25	21.87	06.25	09.37	2.31
	T. T.	35.48	33.33	15.05	04.30	10.75	2.19
7. Teaching pupils to maintain a critical attitude toward material studies	D. of T.	48.64	32.43	05.40	08.10	05.40	1.89
	T. T.	43.00	26.00	21.00	06.00	04.00	2.02
8. Teaching pupils to prepare for classwork	D. of T.	51.51	27.27	15.15	06.06	00.00	1.75
	T. T.	53.19	25.53	05.31	12.76	03.18	1.86
9. Teaching pupils to locate specific problems	D. of T.	60.52	31.58	02.63	02.63	02.63	1.55
	T. T.	50.52	29.47	09.45	08.40	02.10	1.82
10. Teaching pupils to analyze problems	D. of T.	67.56	21.62	10.81	00.00	00.00	1.43
	T. T.	54.54	26.31	11.36	06.81	01.13	1.73
11. Teaching pupils to organize material in proper form	D. of T.	63.63	27.27	06.06	03.03	00.00	1.47
	T. T.	49.41	29.41	12.94	07.17	01.17	1.81
12. Teaching pupils to summarize material	D. of T.	40.54	45.94	05.40	05.40	02.70	1.83
	T. T.	44.08	32.25	17.20	02.15	04.30	1.90
13. Teaching pupils to combine ideas in proper relationship	D. of T.	48.57	25.71	20.00	02.85	02.85	1.85
	T. T.	48.86	29.54	12.50	04.52	04.52	1.86

TABLE XVII (*Continued*)

Group of Activities	Rank	1	2	3	4	5	Average Rank
14. Teaching pupils to discuss implications of material studied	D. of T.	46.66	36.66	03.33	06.66	06.66	1.90
	T. T.	35.16	31.86	19.78	04.39	08.78	2.19
15. Teaching pupils to find or make illustrations for greater clearness	D. of T.	30.30	30.30	33.33	03.03	03.03	2.18
	T. T.	30.23	30.23	18.60	13.95	06.97	2.37
16. Teaching pupils to note, outline, and record useful information	D. of T.	29.41	35.29	17.64	08.82	05.88	2.26
	T. T.	42.22	23.33	15.55	11.11	07.77	2.19
17. Teaching pupils to take tests and examinations efficiently	D. of T.	25.71	28.57	20.00	11.40	11.40	2.22
	T. T.	30.33	20.22	18.00	11.23	20.22	2.70
18. Teaching pupils to compare work with standards in order to check errors	D. of T.	26.46	32.35	17.64	14.70	08.82	2.47
	T. T.	24.70	29.41	23.52	04.68	17.64	2.61
19. Teaching pupils to correct errors	D. of T.	52.92	23.42	11.71	05.88	05.88	1.88
	T. T.	53.40	21.58	09.04	05.68	10.11	2.04
II. Activities Involving Classroom Management and Control							
A. Routine factors							
1. Recording attendance	D. of T.	42.22	15.79	10.52	18.42	13.15	2.44
	T. T.	31.82	14.88	16.53	15.95	25.53	2.84
2. Filling out forms required by the school office	D. of T.	28.57	25.71	14.28	17.14	14.28	2.62
	T. T.	33.00	14.43	18.55	14.43	19.58	2.73
3. Searching for records of individuals	D. of T.	20.00	20.57	17.14	17.14	17.14	2.80
	T. T.	20.65	26.08	23.91	11.95	17.39	2.90
4. Searching for records of class-groups	D. of T.	13.88	19.44	27.76	16.66	22.22	3.13
	T. T.	17.58	26.37	24.17	18.46	15.39	2.85
5. Reporting achievement of class-work	D. of T.	35.13	29.72	16.21	10.81	08.07	2.29
	T. T.	34.02	27.83	18.55	11.34	08.24	2.31
6. Maintaining proper temperature in classroom	D. of T.	52.50	22.50	12.50	02.50	10.00	1.95
	T. T.	56.70	20.51	11.34	01.03	10.26	1.87
7. Securing proper lighting of classroom	D. of T.	57.50	15.00	17.50	02.50	07.50	1.87
	T. T.	58.00	21.00	10.00	01.00	10.00	1.84
8. Care of the ventilation of the classroom	D. of T.	65.79	05.26	15.79	05.26	07.89	1.84
	T. T.	56.00	18.00	11.00	03.00	12.00	1.97
9. Making classroom attractive	D. of T.	39.73	29.21	21.05	10.52	02.63	2.07
	T. T.	38.30	36.17	10.63	07.44	07.44	2.09
10. Making available the supplies for teaching	D. of T.	36.84	21.11	29.21	02.63	10.52	2.29
	T. T.	52.08	26.04	07.29	10.41	04.16	1.88
B. Activities involving pupil and student-teacher relationships							
1. Teaching pupils desirable attitudes and ideals	D. of T.	84.87	12.82	02.56	00.00	00.00	1.25
	T. T.	89.00	05.00	05.00	01.00	00.00	1.18
2. Teaching the school's regulations	D. of T.	27.76	13.88	19.44	22.22	16.66	2.86
	T. T.	23.71	27.83	17.52	17.52	13.40	2.58
3. Rewarding meritorious conduct	D. of T.	35.13	16.21	18.91	16.21	13.51	2.70
	T. T.	18.28	25.80	22.58	15.05	18.28	2.89
4. Penalizing misdemeanors	D. of T.	21.11	15.79	21.11	21.11	21.11	3.05
	T. T.	10.63	17.02	24.46	14.88	32.97	3.42
5. Applying preventive measures in directing children	D. of T.	47.36	29.21	18.42	02.63	02.63	1.57
	T. T.	47.42	26.81	09.27	10.26	06.08	2.01

TABLE XVII (*Continued*)

GROUP OF ACTIVITIES	RANK	RANKED PERCENTAGES					AVER-AGE RANK
		1	2	3	4	5	
6. Respect for the desires and welfare of pupils	D. of T.	51.28	33.58	12.82	00.00	05.12	1.76
	T. T.	57.57	28.28	08.08	03.03	03.03	1.65
7. Teaching pupils to work independently	D. of T.	69.44	16.66	05.55	08.33	00.00	1.50
	T. T.	64.00	19.00	13.00	02.00	02.00	1.59
8. Establishing cordial relationships with pupils	D. of T.	48.64	37.83	02.70	08.10	02.70	1.78
	T. T.	66.00	27.00	04.00	03.00	00.00	1.44
III. *The Student-Teacher's Part in Extra-Class and Community Activities*							
A. Extra-class activities							
1. Assists in planning and directing assembly programs	D. of T.	35.13	27.02	32.43	05.40	00.00	2.07
	T. T.	35.35	29.29	18.18	07.07	10.10	2.27
2. Participates in school campaigns and drives	D. of T.	03.22	16.12	19.35	16.12	45.16	3.83
	T. T.	14.28	31.63	23.46	10.20	20.40	2.80
3. Directs club activities	D. of T.	28.20	41.02	15.38	12.82	02.56	2.20
	T. T.	31.00	38.00	17.00	09.00	05.00	2.19
4. Chaperons groups	D. of T.	05.88	29.41	29.41	17.64	17.64	3.11
	T. T.	11.11	20.20	27.77	14.44	26.66	3.25
5. Takes pupils on excursions	D. of T.	21.62	35.13	24.32	08.07	10.80	2.51
	T. T.	27.15	31.57	21.05	09.45	01.05	2.44
6. Acts as official judge in contests	D. of T.	08.33	11.10	30.55	30.55	19.44	3.41
	T. T.	14.88	23.40	19.14	15.95	26.59	3.15
7. Coaches pupils	D. of T.	10.80	32.43	21.62	18.91	16.21	3.00
	T. T.	25.55	30.00	18.88	10.00	15.55	2.60
B. Community activities							
1. Gives advice and information to parents	D. of T.	36.66	16.66	10.00	16.66	20.00	2.66
	T. T.	36.26	26.37	17.58	06.59	13.18	2.30
2. Meets socially with parents-teachers	D. of T.	12.50	45.00	15.00	07.50	20.00	2.77
	T. T.	46.31	30.52	18.94	02.05	02.05	1.77
3. Participates in parent-teacher meetings	D. of T.	08.57	34.28	28.57	08.57	17.14	2.91
	T. T.	33.70	34.78	20.65	06.12	10.87	2.11
4. Visits commercial and service clubs and organizations of community	D. of T.	03.22	22.22	22.22	25.48	25.48	3.48
	T. T.	19.19	25.29	22.98	20.69	21.81	3.20
5. Establishes contact with church interests	D. of T.	08.82	23.42	17.64	17.64	26.46	3.32
	T. T.	14.13	33.70	25.00	19.56	07.60	2.72
6. Assists in community drives and campaigns	D. of T.	03.08	06.25	15.62	31.25	43.74	4.06
	T. T.	04.34	20.65	23.91	14.13	30.43	3.26
IV. *The Student-Teacher's Growth*							
A. Personal factors							
1. Analysis of personality traits in others	D. of T.	40.54	20.00	20.00	14.28	02.85	2.14
	T. T.	37.00	32.00	24.00	03.00	04.00	2.05
2. Self-analysis of personality	D. of T.	72.22	13.88	08.33	02.77	02.77	1.50
	T. T.	83.83	09.09	07.09	00.00	00.00	1.23
3. Methods devised to improve traits	D. of T.	51.35	29.18	13.51	05.40	00.00	1.73
	T. T.	56.00	37.00	07.00	00.00	00.00	1.51
B. Professional factors							
1. Develop interest in teaching as a profession	D. of T.	84.87	12.82	00.00	02.56	00.00	1.20
	T. T.	82.47	13.40	04.12	00.00	00.00	1.21

TABLE XVII (*Continued*)

GROUP OF ACTIVITIES	RANK	RANKED PERCENTAGES					AVER-AGE RANK
		I	2	3	4	5	
2. Reading of professional periodicals	D. of T.	58.42	29.21	07.89	05.26	00.00	1.60
	T. T.	45.90	28.57	20.40	03.06	01.02	1.83
3. Information given about the best professional organizations	D. of T.	28.71	45.16	16.12	09.66	00.00	2.06
	T. T.	25.53	23.40	20.21	22.33	08.51	2.64
4. Teaching means of "growth in service"	D. of T.	67.56	29.72	02.70	00.00	00.00	1.35
	T. T.	70.10	16.49	06.18	01.03	06.18	1.56

DISTRIBUTION OF ACTIVITIES INTO THREE GROUPS OF IMPORTANCE

An interesting study develops if the one hundred and two activities are listed in the order of their averaged rank, from highest to lowest, as assigned by the directors of training. After such an arrangement, if we arbitrarily assume that the activities falling in the upper third are of greatest importance in the list of the hundred and two activities, those in the middle third of average importance, and those in the lowest third of least importance, we shall be able by this method to locate each activity in its respective group of importance.

Of the thirty-four activities in the group of highest importance, twenty-seven fall in the first large division of the master list, namely, "Activities Involving Class Instruction"; three under "Activities Involving Classroom Management and Control"; none under "The Student's Part in Extra-Class and Community Activities"; and four under "The Student-Teacher's Growth." This bears out the conclusions drawn in a previous chapter that in the descriptions and other printed matter, of courses relating to student-teaching, in catalogues, the chief emphasis is placed on a mastery of classroom technique.

The preponderance of activities listed in the third group that fall under such headings as "The Student-Teacher's Part in Extra-Class and Community Activities" and "Management and Routine" indicates that activities of this nature are considered by these two groups to be of less importance than those listed under "Class Instruction."

Table XVIII gives the activities as they are classified into groups of thirds. These are arranged in order of importance as given by the directors of training.

TABLE XVIII

DISTRIBUTION OF ACTIVITIES IN THE MASTER LIST GROUPED INTO THIRDS

Groups I, II, III Are Considered of Greatest, Average, and Least Importance Respectively, as Rated by the Directors of Training

ACTIVITY	DIRECTORS' AVERAGE SCORE

Group I or activities of greatest importance
1. Develop interest in teaching as a profession 1.20
2. Diagnosing pupil's difficulties and needs 1.20
3. Teaching pupils desirable attitudes and ideals 1.25
4. Teaching pupils to foresee results to be obtained 1.31
5. Mastery of subject-matter taught 1.32
6. Teaching pupils to decide what is to be done 1.35
7. Selecting subject-matter with reference to pupil's needs 1.35
8. Teaching means of "growth in service" 1.35
9. Subject-matter selected on basis of needs of class 1.37
10. Taking into account pupil's abilities in class instruction 1.39
11. Teaching pupils to solve problems 1.41
12. Selecting materials for study 1.42
13. Selecting subject-matter with reference to pupil's abilities ... 1.43
14. Teaching pupils to analyze problems 1.43
15. Teaching pupils to develop traits and habits 1.45
16. Teaching pupils to organize material in proper form 1.47
17. Determining pupil's interest 1.48
18. Follow-up of diagnosis made 1.48
19. Self-analysis of personality 1.50
20. Teaching pupils to work independently 1.50
21. Setting up standards to achieve 1.52
22. Teaching pupils to develop useful interest, worthy motives, and sincere appreciation 1.53
23. Teaching pupils to locate specific problems 1.55
24. Applying preventive measures in directing children 1.57
25. Methods of presentation suitable to subject-matter 1.58
26. Using methods of instruction to develop interest 1.60
27. Organizing subject-matter 1.60
28. Reading of professional periodicals 1.60
29. Planning methods of presentation 1.60
30. Using drill exercises and problems to fix responses 1.62
31. Planning assignments 1.65
32. Selection of materials to be planned 1.66
33. Teaching pupils to make economical use of time 1.66
34. Determining objectives of materials 1.71

Group II or activities of average importance
1. Teaching pupils how to improve skills and abilities 1.72
2. Methods devised to improve traits 1.73
3. Economical use of time 1.74
4. Teaching pupils to prepare for classwork 1.75

TABLE XVIII (*Continued*)

Activity	Directors' Average Score
5. Forming conclusions, summaries	1.75
6. Respect for the desires and welfare of pupils	1.76
7. Teaching pupils to find desired information from reading material	1.76
8. Utilizing objectives selected in teaching subject-matter	1.77
9. Assignments adapted and organized to meet the requirements of course	1.77
10. Establishing cordial relationships with pupils	1.78
11. Teaching pupils to gather reading materials	1.78
12. Recognition of individual differences in making assignments .	1.79
13. Allowing pupils to assume responsibility in class	1.80
14. Teaching pupils to summarize material	1.83
15. Care of the ventilation of the classroom	1.84
16. Teaching pupils to combine ideas in proper relationship	1.85
17. Securing proper lighting of classroom	1.87
18. Teaching pupils to correct errors	1.88
19. Teaching pupils to maintain a critical attitude toward material studied	1.89
20. Teaching pupils to discuss implications of material studied ..	1.90
21. Consideration of sequence of materials to be taught	1.92
22. Determining specific objectives in harmony with the general objectives	1.94
23. Maintaining proper temperature in classroom	1.95
24. Proper balance of pupil-teacher participation in class instruction	1.96
25. Planning participation	2.00
26. Information given about the best professional organizations ..	2.06
27. Making classroom attractive	2.07
28. Assists in planning and directing assembly programs	2.07
29. Teaching pupils to make practical use of materials studied ..	2.09
30. Teaching pupils to develop individual tendencies and abilities	2.11
31. Planning methods of evaluation of pupil's achievements	2.13
32. Analysis of personality traits in others	2.14
33. Evaluating test papers	2.15
34. Preparing tests	2.17

Group III or activities of least importance

1. Teaching pupils to find or make illustrations for greater clearness	2.18
2. Directing club activities	2.20
3. Teaching pupils to take tests and examinations efficiently ...	2.22
4. Teaching pupils to note, outline, and record useful information	2.26
5. Making available the supplies for teaching	2.29
6. Reporting achievement of classwork	2.29
7. Teaching pupils to obtain a proper perspective of the course ..	2.31
8. Using devices for overcoming difficulties	2.34
9. Determining the general objectives for grade and subject ...	2.36

TABLE XVIII (*Continued*)

ACTIVITY	DIRECTORS' AVERAGE SCORE
10. Teaching pupils to plan methods of work	2.36
11. Determining method of evaluation of pupil's needs, abilities, interests	2.39
12. The use of the plan after its preparation	2.42
13. Selecting standardized tests	2.42
14. Recording attendance	2.44
15. Teaching pupils to compare work with standards in order to check errors	2.47
16. Administering tests	2.49
17. Taking pupils on excursions	2.51
18. Filling out forms required by the school office	2.62
19. Giving advice and information to parents	2.66
20. The writing of the plan	2.69
21. Rewarding meritorious conduct	2.70
22. Meeting socially with parents—teachers	2.77
23. Searching for records of individuals	2.80
24. Teaching the school's regulations	2.86
25. Participates in parent-teacher meetings	2.91
26. Coaching pupils	3.00
27. Penalizing misdemeanors	3.05
28. Chaperoning groups	3.11
29. Searching for records of class groups	3.13
30. Establishing contact with church interests	3.32
31. Acting as official judge in contests	3.41
32. Visiting commercial and service clubs and organizations of community	3.48
33. Participating in school campaigns and drives	3.83
34. Assisting in community drives and campaigns	4.06

A STUDY OF DIFFERENCES IN THE EVALUATIONS MADE BY THE TWO GROUPS

It is of interest to note the differences in evaluations made by the two groups when ranking the items of the list. What items were ranked approximately the same by the two groups? A study of the ten activities with a difference in evaluations of .00 to .04 inclusive was made. Most of the ten fall in the groups of first or second importance. The activity "Develop interest in teaching as a profession" is given first place both by directors of training and training-teachers, the difference of their average rank being .01. Three other activities in this list (see numbers 4, 5, 9 in Table XIX) are related to the planning of subject-matter for teaching purposes.

TABLE XIX

THE TEN ACTIVITIES SHOWING GREATEST AGREEMENT IN THE JUDGMENTS
GIVEN BY THE DIRECTORS OF TRAINING AND THE
TRAINING-TEACHERS

ACTIVITY	DIRECTORS' SCORE	TRAINING-TEACHERS' SCORE	DIFFERENCE	GROUP (FROM TABLE XVIII)
1. Directs club activities ..	2.20	2.19	.01	III
2. Teaching pupils to develop traits and habits	1.45	1.44	.01	I
3. Teaching pupils to combine ideas in proper relationship	1.85	1.86	.01	II
4. Organizing subject-matter	1.60	1.61	.01	I
5. Methods of presentation suitable to subject-matter	1.58	1.59	.01	I
6. Develop interest in teaching as a profession	1.20	1.21	.01	I
7. Reporting achievement of classwork	2.29	2.31	.02	III
8. Making classroom attractive	2.07	2.09	.02	II
9. Utilizing objectives selected in teaching subject-matter	1.77	1.80	.03	II
10. Securing proper lighting of classroom	1.87	1.84	.03	II

In a group of the ten activities showing greatest differences in the evaluations made by the two groups, it is of interest to note that the item "Meets socially with parents-teachers" is ranked by the training-teachers higher by 1.00 than by the directors of training. The item "Determining the general objectives for grade and subject" is ranked by the training-teachers more important by .96 points than by the directors of training. Items ranked higher by the directors of training than by the training-teachers are: "Using drill exercises and problems to fix responses," "Assignments adapted and organized to meet the requirements of course," and "Information given about the best professional organizations." (See numbers 3, 9, 10 in Table XX.)

Directors of training show a greater tendency than do the training-teachers to rank those activities of the nature of classroom

TABLE XX

A Group of the Ten Activities, Showing Least Agreement in the Judgments Given by Directors of Training and the Training-Teachers

Activity	Directors' Score	Training-Teachers' Score	Difference	Group (From Table XVIII)
1. Meets socially with parents-teachers	2.77	1.77	1.00	III
2. Determining the general objectives for grade and subject	2.36	1.40	0.96	III
3. Using drill exercises and problems to fix responses	1.62	2.49	0.87	I
4. Determining method of evaluation of pupil's needs, abilities, interests	2.39	1.56	0.83	III
5. Assists in community drives and campaigns	4.06	3.26	0.80	III
6. Participates in parent-teacher meetings	2.91	2.11	0.80	III
7. Teaching pupils to plan methods of work	2.36	1.56	0.80	III
8. Establishes contact with church interests	3.32	2.72	0.60	III
9. Assignments adapted and organized to meet the requirements of course	1.77	2.36	0.59	II
10. Information given about the best professional organizations	2.06	2.64	0.58	II

techniques as of more importance. On the other hand, the training-teachers rank higher those activities of an extra-class nature in which the social relationships of the student-teacher are involved. The directors of training consider administrative problems of greater importance than do the training-teachers. These different points of view of the two groups are to be expected, in view of the fact that their contact with the work of the course is slightly different. The training-teachers are more intimately associated with the student-teachers than are the directors of training, and for that reason feel the importance and need of the student-teacher's social training. Because of the administrative responsibilities of the directors of training it is reasonable to expect them to consider organization and administration problems as of greater importance in the student-teacher's training.

RELIABILITY OF THE EVALUATIONS OF DIRECTORS OF TRAINING AND TRAINING-TEACHERS

It is desirable at this point to consider the reliability of the evaluations made by the two groups, the directors of training and the training-teachers. It should be said that little has been done by statistical experts in treating judgment scores. The most extensive treatment of such scores is *The Commonwealth Teacher-Training Study*,[1] in which it was found that "twenty-five returns are sufficiently reliable to draw conclusions. In each instance, in the Commonwealth study, the correlations were high, usually in excess of .900.

In determining the reliability of the evaluations made in this study and of the correlations between the ratings by the two juries, three computations were made. The first computation determined the reliability of the evaluations of the directors of training. This result was found by computing the correlation of the averages between random halves of this group. The result showed the correlation to be .8295. This high correlation leads to the conclusion that the reliability of the evaluations of the directors of training is substantial.

The second computation determined the reliability of the evaluations made by the training-teachers. The method used in determining the reliability of the average ratings made by the directors of training was followed. This correlation was found to be .8617, a correlation higher by .0322 than that in the case of the directors of training.

The third computation was a determination of the correlation between the evaluations made by the directors of training with those made by the training-teachers. The resulting coefficient of correlation was .8196. This high correlation between the two groups of judges is further evidence in support of the statement that the evaluations employed in this study are substantially reliable.

It is therefore concluded that the evaluations given in the tables represent reliable and consistent judgments by the directors of

[1] Charters, W. W., and Waples, Douglas, *The Commonwealth Teacher-Training Study*, p. 28.

training and the training-teachers. The high statistical reliability is due to the following facts: first, that the ratings represent
the average judgments of an intelligent group of persons; and
second, that each person agrees closely with the other members in
the groups on the ratings assigned.

The validity of these data is claimed on the following grounds:
first, those coöperating in the study represent two groups of
specialists who, because of superior training and intimate contact
with the student-teaching course, are in a position to give sound
opinions; second, the data represent a sufficiently large sampling,
representative of the whole United States, to give an accurate picture of student-teaching in the state teachers colleges; third, the
judgments recorded by both groups are consistent and reasonable;
and fourth, the judgments of the two juries in this study closely
correlate with the judgments given by the juries in the Commonwealth study in their evaluation of the same items.

A DETERMINATION AS TO WHERE THE SUBJECT-MATTER RELATED TO THE ACTIVITIES IS TAUGHT

In a preceding discussion the conclusion was drawn that student-
teaching activities are carried on almost entirely by the group set
aside for this purpose, namely, the staff of the training department. It seems reasonable to believe, however, that the content
that may be studied in connection with these activities may be
taught in courses other than those in student-teaching. It is con-
ceivable that such activities as "Objectives of grades and subjects," "Methods of instruction to develop interest," "Development
of personality traits," "Develop interest in teaching as a profession," might well be taught in connection with subject-matter and
education courses. If such is the practice, the content of the student-teaching course which follows will be influenced and modified, since the student will have a different background as he enters
the work of teaching.

In connection with the above concept, two lines of inquiries were
followed. First, Is the subject-matter of these activities taught
in connection with subject-matter and education courses? Second,
Should the subject-matter of these activities be taught in connection
with such courses? Although the data would have been more
reliable if subject-matter teachers had been asked these questions
since it involves their teaching, it seemed possible that the directors

of training, in view of their close contact with subject-matter teachers, could give reliable information concerning this problem. The following summarized statements indicate practices and opinions in this regard as revealed by the responses of the directors of training.

Group of Activities	Are Taught in Subject-Matter Courses	Should Be Taught in Subject-Matter Courses
	%	%
1. Activities involving class instruction	10	40
2. Activities involving classroom management and control	8	20
3. The student's part in extra-class and community activities	4	20
4. The student's personal and professional growth	8	15

From the above summary it appears that little is done in the matter of teaching the materials related to these activities in connection with subject-matter courses, and that a considerable number of directors of training favor the policy of teaching these activities in connection with the subject-matter courses.

In the case of education courses, the answers given by the directors would be more reliable since the directors are more closely related to the work of these courses. In 20 per cent of the cases the director of training is also the head of the department of education, as was pointed out in Chapter II. The following summarized statements indicate the practices and opinions in regard to this policy.

Group of Activities	Are Taught in Education Courses	Should Be Taught in Education Courses
	%	%
1. Activities involving class instruction	100	100
2. Activities involving classroom management and control	40	70
3. The student's participation in extra-class and community activities ...	40	60
4. The student's personal and professional growth	100	100

The above data show that all the directors of training are agreed that the education courses are teaching and should teach the subject-matter concerning the "activities involving class instruction" and those concerning "the student's personal and professional growth." They believe, however, that more attention should be given in these courses to the teaching of the subject-matter relating to those "activities involving management and routine" and "extra-class and community activities."

SUMMARY

After the major activities of the course had been determined, it was desirable to find out the relative importance of each activity in the program of student-teaching. With this thought in mind, the activities were submitted to two groups, the directors of training and the training-teachers, who registered their judgments as to the degree of importance which each activity has in the course. The reliability of these evaluations was statistically determined by correlating the two group judgments.

1. After the activities had been evaluated and the averages determined, the list was arranged according to distribution, and then divided into three equal groups. Those falling in the upper third of the distribution were arbitrarily accorded first rank, as of greatest importance; those falling in the middle third of the distribution, as of average importance; and those falling in the lowest third, as of least importance. The conclusions drawn earlier, that the chief emphasis in the courses is placed on a mastery of the techniques of teaching, seem well founded in view of the fact that of the thirty-six activities included in Group I recorded as greatest in importance, twenty-nine are grouped in the master list under the heading "Activities Involving Class Instruction." In the third group (that of least importance) activities of the nature of extra-class, management, and routine predominate.

2. Although the evaluations of both groups show high correlation (as will be pointed out later), it is of interest to note the activities upon which there was greatest and least agreement by the two groups. In general, the activities rated higher by the training teachers were under extra-class and the general objectives of grade and subject; whereas the directors ranked drill devices, the technique of assignments, and professional growth higher than did the training-teachers.

3. The reliability of the evaluations made by the directors of training, determined by the computation of the correlation between random halves of their average scores, showed the high positive correlation of .8295. The reliability of the evaluations made by the training-teacher, determined in the same manner, showed a high positive correlation of .8617, a correlation higher by .032 than that of the directors of training. The correlation between the average scores of the two groups was .8196. Because of the high positive correlations found, it is concluded that the activities selected for the master list are of major importance in the course in student-teaching, and that the judgments given are highly reliable.

Validity is claimed for these data on the ground that the judgments of the two juries represent expert opinion, that a sufficient sampling was secured to give an accurate picture of the institutions of the country, and that the juries were consistent and reasonable in recording their judgments.

4. The judgments of the directors of training, with regard to the policy of teaching in the subject-matter courses the materials related to the activities of student-teaching, are probably not as reliable as the judgments of the subject-matter teachers would be. Yet, in view of the directors' close contact with subject-matter teachers, their answers to this inquiry may be relied upon with some degree of certainty. These officers indicate that this policy is not the practice in their institutions, and evidently they do not believe that such should be followed. Only one-third of the group favored such a policy, and then only in the case of the activities which fall under techniques of class instruction. In their judgment such teaching is done in connection with education courses, and rightly so.

CHAPTER V

SUMMARY, CONCLUSIONS, AND RECOMMENDATIONS

The main issues of this study should be considered in the light of present-day conditions as they exist in the state teachers colleges of this country. The conclusions drawn, the supporting evidence, and the recommendations made have specific bearing and relationship to the problem of training teachers for the secondary school service. The data secured and the recommendations made are confined entirely to the practices in state teachers colleges.

Because of the wide range of practices in the organization of the courses in student-teaching, it is evident that the teachers colleges do not agree on any group of guiding principles that should govern the work in student-teaching, particularly on the secondary level. This situation is due, as may be expected, to the rapid changes in so short a time in these institutions. This lack of uniformity may be desirable in view of the fact that so many different local and state conditions have to be met.

The need for a determination of the activities of student-teaching courses and for an evaluation to be made in terms of successful teaching service is great, since there are such divergent practices in the organization and content of the courses. A determination of the major activities and of their relative importance should be of assistance to the training staff inasmuch as it will show what activity should be taught and where emphasis should be placed. It will also be helpful in defining more clearly the underlying principles that should govern the program of student-teaching.

CONCLUSIONS

A. REGARDING THE ORGANIZATION OF THE INSTITUTION FOR STUDENT-TEACHING

1. *The assumption that the organization of the state teachers colleges for student-teaching definitely influences the content of the courses is, in general, confirmed.*

(1) The availability of laboratory facilities for student-teaching activities is one of the factors determining the content of the major activities of the course. Where there is a lack of laboratory facilities, observation and participation are increased and teaching activities are decreased.

(2) There is sufficient evidence to show that more time is given to student-teaching activities, particularly to actual teaching of classwork, if the ratio between high school pupils and college students is increased.

(3) Where there is lack of facilities for student-teaching, there is a tendency to increase the service load of the training-teachers. In some cases these teachers are supervising as many as thirty student-teachers during a term, or from four to six students during one class period.

(4) The assumption is made that the background of the student prior to assignment to student-teaching modifies the work of the course in view of his lack of knowledge of the materials he is to teach. The data show that the median case in the distribution showing amount of work required before teaching is twenty semester-hours, Q_1 being approximately twelve semester-hours, and Q_3 being approximately thirty semester-hours. These facts indicate that in fully one-third of the colleges, student-teaching work is assigned to students who have had less than two years of college work in the subject-matter they must teach. We have no scientific evidence to show that students profit as much, or become as skillful teachers, when they have had limited background in their major field of interest prior to the student-teaching experience as when they have had an extra amount of such training. But it is reasonable to believe that the content of the course in student-teaching will of necessity be modified to meet the requirements of all types of organizations.

(5) The range in the amount of college credit given for the course in student-teaching shows the widely diverse opinions held by the various institutions with regard to the value of the student-teaching work in the training of teachers. The common practice is to give from 8 to 10 semester-hours credit for the course; the range, however, is from 3 to 45 semester-hours. In the institutions where little credit is given for the course, time is reduced for the various activities, and usually the amount of class teaching suffers most in this reduction.

(6) From the data secured it appears that the institutions are, in general, organized with little thought of integrating the work of all the forces of the institution. The training departments are usually held responsible for the work of student-teaching, the other departments having little or no responsibilities for this work. This inquiry was made because of the fact that so much has been written with regard to the professionalization of the institution's activities. If all of the instructional staff have responsibilities in professionalizing the work taught, it seems reasonable to believe that the course in student-teaching would be vitally influenced by such a policy. We may conclude that this is not the general practice, and that the activities in the course are taught largely in education and student-teaching courses.

B. REGARDING THE ORGANIZATION OF THE COURSE IN STUDENT-TEACHING

1. *The general activities of the course in student-teaching are: observation, participation, teaching, preparation, conferences, extra-class, and management and routine. Judging from the evaluations of the data secured, the general activities of primary importance are: observation, participation, teaching, and conferences. Extra-class, management and routine activities occupy a place of secondary importance.*

2. *There is no common practice with regard to the amount of time that is given to each activity in the course.*

(1) Although the median number of hours in observation is 15% of the total time, the range is from 2.5% to 50%. The median institution provides 38% of the time for teaching activities; the range is from 10% to 80%. The time provided for the other types of activities varies from one institution to another and shows the same fluctuating tendency.

(2) From an analysis of the time allotments provided for the various activities, it is clear that the content of the course in student-teaching in some institutions may be composed largely of classroom teaching.

(3) There were insufficient data from which to draw conclusions with regard to the time given to management and routine problems. Such activities are usually incidental. The data show, however, that students have responsibilities in these matters. The check list, evaluated by the directors of training and by the train-

ing-teachers, indicates that student-teachers are trained in such work but that such activities are of secondary importance and are given less emphasis by those administering the course.

3. *A study of catalogues, manuals, syllabi, rating cards, and descriptive bulletins indicates that the course is organized so as to give major emphasis to those activities involved in classroom instruction. The evaluations of the activities of the check list by the two groups support this same conclusion.*

4. *The content of the conference, considered a vital part of the course by all the directors of training coöperating in this study, consists of: discussions of the techniques of teaching employed by the student-teacher in classwork, criticisms of the student's execution of the techniques used in teaching, improvement of the student's personality traits, and the development of a professional point of view.*

C. REGARDING THE MAJOR ACTIVITIES OF THE COURSE AS REVEALED BY AN ACTIVITY ANALYSIS

1. *Although not exhaustive, the master list of activities evolved represents the major activities of the course in student-teaching designed to train secondary teachers.*

Although the directors of training and the training-teachers were asked to supplement the list with additional activities which, in their judgment, should be added to make the list complete, only twenty-three additional activities were suggested. In many of the activities added there was decided overlapping with the master list evolved.

2. *The evaluations made by the two groups, the directors of training and the training-teachers, of the activities in the master list are reliable and provide definite evidence as to the degrees of value of each activity in the course in student-teaching.*

(1) Statistical treatment of the evaluations made by the directors of training resulted in the high positive correlation of .8295 between random halves, a correlation substantial enough to indicate that the judgments of this group are highly reliable.

(2) The high positive correlation of .8617 between random halves of the evaluations made by the training-teachers provides definite evidence that their judgments are highly reliable.

3. *Because of the high correlation between the ratings of one group as compared with the other, it is concluded that there is sub-stantial agreement between the two groups as to the value of the activities in the student-teaching program.*

The positive correlation between the judgments of the two groups was .8196.

4. *The location of each activity as to value provides reliable information with regard to the emphasis that is given to the activities of the course, as it is at present organized.*

By arranging the activities in a descending scale of distribution, and arbitrarily dividing the activities into three even groups, we are able to determine where the emphasis is now placed in the course. An analysis of these data indicates that the emphasis is placed on two general types of activities, namely: those involving classroom instruction and those involving the student's personal and professional growth.

5. *The subject-matter of the activities of the master list is not taught in connection with subject-matter courses, generally speaking; and in the judgment of the directors of training, this policy should not be followed. This practice is reversed in the case of education courses.*

RECOMMENDATIONS

In view of the fact that the practices and policies affecting the student-teaching program are so variable in the state teachers colleges of the nation, there is definite need to evolve a body of guiding principles that should govern this work. Several pertinent questions need to be answered in determining such principles, however. Among such are: What is the relative value of observation as compared to teaching? How are teaching skills developed? May skills be developed through observation alone? Are the claims, often made, that student-teaching is designed largely to develop teaching skills, valid? What is student-teaching? Is it a combination of all the major activities of teaching, or may it be composed entirely of observation or teaching? We have little scientific evidence to answer the above questions.

The assumption has been made that the skills in teaching are developed through practice in their use in actual situations. Reason seems to guide us in such a belief, and personal observations seem to substantiate the belief. Experiments should be conducted to provide reliable evidence in support of this judgment or belief. So varied are the judgments of the experts in this field that their opinions are often radically opposed on issues which are considered most fundamental. The need for answers to many perplexing and unanswered problems related to the program of student-teaching offers a tremendous challenge to those engaged in this work.

A. REGARDING THE ORGANIZATION AND ADMINISTRATION OF THE INSTITUTIONS FOR TEACHER-TRAINING

In the study of the organization of the institutions it was pointed out that the subject-matter, education, and teacher-training departments are administered in such a way that their functions are not integrated, but operate parallel to one another. The work of student-teaching is done almost exclusively by a staff set aside for this purpose. Since the ultimate objective of every staff member, regardless of department, should be to train effective teachers for the secondary school service, each should be well informed with regard to the training the institution provides, to the end that the work may be professionally integrated and unified. In such an organization the student would receive training that is continuous and related, all functioning toward a definite goal.

In order to promote closer coördination of all the college interests, the following recommendations are made:

1. The institution should be organized and administered in such way that the work of all the interests of the college is coördinated and integrated.

   (1) There should be a highly trained specialist in coördination, who has broad training in subject-matter and education and is experienced in administration, to serve as a coordinator of all the institution's activities. This person may be the dean of instruction or some other person designated to do this superior type of work. His chief function is to assist and direct the activities that lead toward coördination through institutional agencies.

   (2) A council, or a committee, on coördination should be formed representing all the college interests. The chief purposes of such a council are to devise ways and means of co-

ordinating the various interests of the institution, to arrive at working principles, and to keep the objectives of the institution's program of training before the staff members.

(3) The education and teacher-training departments should be organized under one departmental organization with one person designated as the head or director of the activities of both divisions. The union of the two interests under one head would have a tendency to integrate the activities of these two departments; hence it would reduce the number of conflicting purposes to a minimum.

(4) The work of teacher-training, although administered by a head of the department, should be considered an integral part of all the departments of the college. All are engaged in preparing teachers for high school service; hence, all should have a part in promoting, directing, and supervising the activities of the students trained in subject-matter and education under their teaching.

   a. Heads of departments and their staff members should assist in the supervision of student-teaching. All work in supervision should be carried on coöperatively between subject-matter teachers and teachers of subjects in education. The work, administered by a director of student-teaching, becomes the climax of the training given by all staff members.

   b. Subject-matter teachers and teachers of education should have responsibility in demonstration teaching in the high school grades of the training or demonstration school. This contact would place the teachers of subject-matter and the teachers of education in close touch with actual high school conditions, and would tend to develop a sensitiveness to the needs and requirements of the service for which they are preparing teachers.

   c. The regular training school staff should make similar contacts with the college in the teaching of college classes. This interrelationship becomes mutually helpful to all concerned.

(5) Separate schools should be operated for observation-demonstration-experimentation and student-teaching. The work of one type of school interferes with the work of the other, if both are carried on in the same institution. One should be

used to demonstrate the theories advocated by staff members, to verify such theories by experimentation, and to observe various tendencies in secondary education. Other schools should be used for student-teaching.

(6) The demonstration school should be easily accessible to all staff members of all departments of the college in order that subject-matter and education courses may have demonstrations for purposes of professionalization.

If the institution is organized on such a basis, with student-teaching as the climax or culmination of all the efforts, with all the staff members having a definite part in the entire program, it then occupies a strategic position in the program of training. The chief objective of all has been to develop a well-prepared teacher; the testing of the program is accomplished under actual teaching conditions.

B. REGARDING THE INSTITUTIONAL POLICIES AND THE FACILITIES FOR STUDENT-TEACHING

The following recommendations are made in view of the fact that the evidence supports the conclusion that the content of student-teaching courses is definitely influenced by the requirements which the institutions have established in their provision for adequate laboratory facilities.

1. The minimum laboratory facilites should be increased to the level advocated by Learned, Bagley, and others,[1] of four pupils to one college senior enrolled. The limitations of facilities would not then be the determining factor in deciding whether the course should be observation, participation, or teaching. The needs of the student may then be made the determining factor in deciding what is best for the students rather than the limitations of laboratory facilities.

(1) This increase in facilities would be met in different ways by the various institutions. Some would find it necessary to increase the present campus schools; in other cases, city and town high schools may be used to care for such increases.

(2) As has been stated, the demonstration and student-teaching programs would not be operated in the same school.

[1] Learned, W. S. and Bagley, W. C., and Others, *The Professional Preparation of Teachers for American Public Schools*, p. 193-195.

2. Sufficient time and college credit should be allowed for the courses in student-teaching in order that teaching skills may have a chance to be developed and definite desirable teaching habits established.

(1) For the typical student a specified time limit should be placed upon the course in student-teaching. There are exceptions, in which cases it would be desirable to require more hours of teaching or fewer hours of teaching, depending upon the needs of the student. When the standard of efficiency that the institution has set up as being desirable has been met by the student, he should be excused from the course and certified to teach.

(2) College credit should be given, with certain limitations, in proportion to the time devoted to the course. A minimum requirement of credit may be made and limitations placed upon a maximum amount to be given. Beyond this maximum the student would work without college credit.

3. The training in subject-matter and education courses should be sufficient to insure broad training in the fields of subject-matter that the student must teach, as well as in related fields. Such training should give the student sufficient margin to enable him to give his time to the mastery of the skills in teaching rather than to an expenditure of his time in learning the subject-matter to be taught.

(1) A minimum of thirty semester-hours in the field of subject-matter that the student-teacher is to teach should be the minimum prerequisite requirement for assignment to student-teaching experience.

(2) Student-teaching should be postponed to a time as late as possible in the course, preferably until the senior year. This requirement would allow for greater maturity in the student, and broader training as prerequisite to the course in student-teaching. This recommendation is based on the assumption that the baccalaureate degree or four years of college training should be the minimum preparation for certification to teach in the secondary school.

4. The professional status, salary, and service-load, including

supervisory responsibilities, of the training teacher, should be on the same level as that of other staff members.

(1) Broad training, the minimum of the A.M. degree, and rich teaching experience should be the minimum requirement for demonstration teaching and supervision.

(2) There should be no distinction in salary and professional status between training-teachers and college staff members, provided the background of each group is equal.

(3) In line with the suggestions made in the next division of recommendations, not more than one student-teacher should be assigned to a training-teacher at one given time.

The author is fully aware of the implications regarding the facilities for teaching that are made in the above recommendations, considering present practices and present conditions. With the facilities now available, the above suggested organization could not be carried out except in a few cases. These recommendations would mean large increases in laboratory facilities in many cases, but in view of the great need for teacher-training such expansion is justifiable.

C. ACTIVITIES OF THE COURSE IN STUDENT-TEACHING

No suggestions are made with regard to the activities in the master list, which was checked by directors of training and training-teachers. This list is sufficiently complete to insure a well trained teacher for the high school, provided the student-teacher is given sufficient opportunity to develop skill in the performance of each of the activities. The author believes, however, aside from the training given in the techniques of teaching, that too little emphasis is placed on activities other than classroom teaching; that training in classroom teaching represents only one portion of the ideal program of training. An analysis of current literature in the field of secondary education bears out this point of view.

The following recommendations are made in view of this apparent need for broader training.

1. The student-teacher should be assigned work that carries all the responsibilities that the regular teacher assumes, thus assuring a type of training that will equip him to carry on successfully

these activities when he becomes a regularly employed high school teacher.

    a. The student-teacher should have training in management and routine problems, including discipline, to the end that he may be equipped to solve such problems after employment in a teaching situation.

    b. In view of the emphasis placed on extra-class activities by the high schools, it is recommended that the student-teaching program should provide opportunities for the student to develop skill in promoting and directing activities of this nature.

It is not only important that the students who later teach in the high schools be well informed about extra-class activities but they should be prepared to direct such activities successfully upon employment. The logical time and place in the curriculum for this training to be given is in connection with the student-teaching course, during the time contacts are made with high school pupils. A few statements from known leaders in the field of secondary education support the statement that these activities are of vital importance in high school work, and that teachers in this field have definite responsibility in directing them.

As early as 1918, Dr. Alexander Inglis, in writing about the importance of extra-class activities stated:

Beyond question secondary education should encompass the extra-curriculum activities and, as far as possible, bring them within the scope of secondary school organization.[2]

Dr. Leonard V. Koos, in discussing allied activities or extra-class activities in the high school organization, states:

There can be no doubt that they have been making increasing demands on the student, on the members of the high school staff, and even on the community. That they are looming in importance in the minds of educational workers is attested by increasing attention to them in educational periodicals and in educational conventions and teachers' meetings, where problems of the secondary school come up for discussion.[3]

[2] Inglis, Alexander, *Principles of Secondary Education,* p. 716.
[3] Koos, Leonard V., *The American Secondary School,* p. 583.

Calvin O. Davis, in discussing what he termed collateral activities of the junior high school, stated:

Every junior high school should make adequate provisions for collateral activities in the fields of art, music, oratory, dramatic art, athletics, social recreations, and community service. General student organizations should be fostered and protected and the growth of helpful clubs encouraged.[4]

Dr. Isaac L. Kandel, in a recent book (1931) in which he discussed the development of extra-class activities, stated:

To the expansion of the high school programs must be added the remarkable development of extra-curricular activities to promote extra-scholastic interests of the pupils. So important have these become that a special body of literature has grown up on the subject, and teachers specially trained in them are employed to lead, guide, and supervise them.[5]

D. REGARDING THE PROFESSIONALIZATION OF SUBJECT-MATTER
COURSES AS IT RELATES TO THE COURSE IN STUDENT-TEACHING

The observations made by the author, of situations in which the subject-matter is professionalized, lead him to believe that through this method of treatment of subject-matter materials the content of student-teaching courses is definitely influenced and modified. He was unable to secure sufficient data to draw reliable conclusions with regard to this policy. He therefore recommends that studies be conducted that would give scientific evidence of the value of this method of subject-matter treatment with particular emphasis on its relationship to the courses in student-teaching.

[4] Davis, Calvin O., *Junior High School Education*, p. 353.
[5] Kandel, Isaac L., *History of Secondary Education*, p. 474.

APPENDIX A

INSTITUTIONS COÖPERATING IN THE QUESTION-NAIRE STUDY

Institution	No. Directors of Training	No. Training Teachers
1. Alabama		
State Teachers College, Jacksonville	0	2
2. Arizona		
State Teachers College, Flagstaff	1	0
State Teachers College, Tempe	1	0
3. California		
State Teachers College, Fresno	1	0
State Teachers College, San Diego	1	0
State Teachers College, San Francisco ...	1	0
4. Colorado		
State Teachers College, Greeley	1	14
5. Georgia		
State Woman's College, Valdosta	1	0
6. Illinois		
Southern Illinois State Teachers College, Carbondale	1	0
Eastern Illinois State Teachers College, Charleston	1	0
Western Illinois State Teachers College, Macomb	1	3
7. Iowa		
State Teachers College, Cedar Falls	1	3
8. Kansas		
State Teachers College, Emporia	1	0
State Teachers College, Hays	1	0
State Teachers College, Pittsburg	1	0
9. Kentucky		
Western Kentucky State Teachers College, Bowling Green	0	3
State Teachers College, Morehead	0	2
State Teachers College, Murray	0	1
Eastern Kentucky State Teachers College, Richmond	1	1
10. Louisiana		
State Teachers College, Lafayette	1	1

Institution	No. Directors of Training	No. Training Teachers
11. Michigan		
State Normal College, Ypsilanti	1	1
12. Minnesota		
State Teachers College, Bernidge	1	0
13. Missouri		
State Teachers College, Cape Girardeau ..	0	1
State Teachers College, Maryville	1	0
State Teachers College, Springfield	1	0
14. Nebraska		
State Teachers College, Peru	1	0
State Teachers College, Wayne	0	1
15. New Jersey		
State Teachers College, Montclair	1	22
State Teachers College, Trenton	1	0
16. New Mexico		
New Mexico Normal University, Las Vegas	1	0
17. New York		
State Teachers College, Buffalo	1	0
Teachers College, Columbia University, New York City	0	11
18. North Carolina		
State Teachers College, Boone	1	0
North Carolina College for Women, Greensboro	1	0
State Teachers College, Greenville	1	1
19. North Dakota		
State Teachers College, Mayville	1	0
20. Ohio		
Ohio University, Athens	0	2
State College, Bowling Green	1	0
Kent State College, Kent	0	1
21. Oklahoma		
State Teachers College, Ada	0	1
State Teachers College, Durant	1	0
State Teachers College, Tahlequah	1	0
State Teachers College, Weatherford	0	2
22. Pennsylvania		
State Teachers College, Bloomsburg	1	0
State Teachers College, E. Stroudsburg ..	1	1
State Teachers College, Lock Haven	1	0
State Teachers College, Millersville	1	0
State Teachers College, Shippensburg	0	1
State Teachers College, Slippery Rock ...	1	0
23. South Carolina		
Winthrop College, Rock Hill	1	0

INSTITUTION	No. DIRECTORS OF TRAINING	No. TRAINING TEACHERS
24. South Dakota		
State Teachers College, Springfield	1	0
25. Tennessee		
State Teachers College, Johnson City	1	0
State Teachers College, Murfreesboro	1	0
Peabody College, Nashville	0	14
26. Texas		
State Teachers College, Commerce	1	3
State Teachers College, Denton	1	2
State Teachers College, Huntsville	1	0
State Teachers College, San Marcos	1	0
27. Virginia		
State Teachers College, East Radford ...	1	0
State Teachers College, Harrisonburg	1	4
28. Washington		
State Normal College, Cheney	0	2
29. West Virginia		
Normal College, Athens	1	0
State Teachers College, Fairmont	1	0
Marshall College, Huntington	1	0
30. Wisconsin		
State Teachers College, Milwaukee	1	0
State Teachers College, Plattville	1	0
State Teachers College, River Falls	1	0
State Teachers College, Stevens Point ...	1	0
State Teachers College, Superior	1	0
	55	100

APPENDIX B

LIST OF INSTITUTIONS INCLUDED IN THE CATALOGUE STUDY

Institution	Year
1. Alabama	
State Teachers College, Florence	1930–31
State Teachers College, Troy	1930–31
2. Arizona	
State Teachers College, Flagstaff	1931–32
State Teachers College, Tempe	1930–31
3. Arkansas	
State Teachers College, Conway	1931
State Teachers College, Henderson	1930
4. California	
State Teachers College, Fresno	1931–32
State Teachers College, San Diego	1930–31
5. Colorado	
State Teachers College, Greeley	1931–32
6. Georgia	
Southern Georgia Teachers College, Collegeboro	1930–31
State Woman's College, Valdosta	1930–31
7. Illinois	
State Teachers College, Charleston	1931–32
State Teachers College, De Kalb	1930–31
State Teachers College, Macomb	1930–31
State Teachers College, Normal	1931–32
8. Indiana	
State Teachers College, Monroe	1930–31
State Teachers College, Terre Haute	1930–31
9. Iowa	
State Teachers College, Cedar Falls	
10. Kansas	
State Teachers College, Emporia	1930–31
State Teachers College, Pittsburg	1930–31
11. Kentucky	
State Teachers College, Morehead	1930–31
State Teachers College, Murray	1931–32
State Teachers College, Richmond	1930–31
12. Louisiana	
State Teachers College, Nachitoches	1931

13. Michigan
    State Normal College, Kalamazoo 1931–32
    State Teachers College, Mount Pleasant 1930–31
    State Teachers College, Ypsilanti 1930–31
14. Minnesota
    State Teachers College, Mankato 1931–32
    State Teachers College, Saint Cloud 1931–32
    State Teachers College, Winona 1930–31
15. Mississippi
    State Teachers College, Cleveland 1931–32
16. Missouri
    State Teachers College, Springfield 1930–32
    State Teachers College, Warrensburg 1930–31
17. Nebraska
    State Teachers College, Chadron 1930–31
    State Teachers College, Peru 1930–31
    State Teachers College, Kearney 1931–32
18. New Jersey
    State Teachers College, Montclair 1931–32
19. New York
    State Teachers College, Albany 1931–32
    State Teachers College, Buffalo 1931–32
20. North Dakota
    State Teachers College, Mayville 1931–32
    State Teachers College, Minot 1930–31
21. Ohio
    State Teachers College, Athens 1930–31
    State Teachers College, Cleveland 1930–31
    State Teachers College, Kent 1931–32
22. Oklahoma
    State Teachers College, Ada 1930–31
    State Teachers College, Alva 1930–31
    State Teachers College, Durant 1930–31
    State Teachers College, Tahlequah 1930–31
23. Pennsylvania
    State Teachers College, Indiana 1931–32
    State Teachers College, Slippery Rock 1930–31
24. South Dakota
    State Teachers College, Aberdeen 1930–31
    State Teachers College, Springfield 1931
25. Tennessee
    State Teachers College, Johnson City 1930
26. Texas
    State Teachers College, Canyon 1930–31
    State Teachers College, Commerce 1930–31
    State Teachers College, Denton 1930–31
    State Teachers College, San Marcos 1930–31

78 *Content of Student-Teaching Courses*

Institution	Year

27. Virginia
    State Teachers College, East Radford 1931–32
    State Teachers College, Fredericksburg 1931–32
    State Teachers College, Harrisonburg 1930–31
28. Wisconsin
    State Teachers College, La Cross 1931
    State Teachers College, Oshkosh 1930–31
    State Teachers College, Platteville 1930–31
    State Teachers College, River Falls 1930

BIBLIOGRAPHY

AGNEW, WALTER DEE. *The Administration of Professional Schools for Teachers.* Baltimore, Warwick and York, 1924.

ALEXANDER, THOMAS. *The Training of Elementary Teachers in Germany.* Studies of the International Institute, No. 5. New York, Teachers College, Columbia University, 1929.

AMERICAN ASSOCIATION OF TEACHERS COLLEGES. *Year-book*, 1923, 1924, 1925, 1926, 1928, 1929.

ARMENTROUT, WINFIELD DOCKERY. *The Conduct of Student Teaching in State Teachers Colleges.* Greeley, Colorado State Teachers College, 1927.

BAGLEY, WILLIAM CHANDLER. "The Distinction between Academic and Professional Subjects." In *N.E.A. Proceedings*, 1918, pp. 229-234.

BAGLEY, WILLIAM CHANDLER. "The Nation's Debt to the Normal Schools." In *Educational Administration and Supervision*, vol. 7, pp. 195-204, 1921.

BAGLEY, WILLIAM CHANDLER. "Professionalism in Education." In *Teachers College Record*, vol. 26, pp. 1-12, January 1924.

BAGLEY, WILLIAM CHANDLER AND OTHERS. *Report of the Survey Commission on the Teacher-Training Institutions of Louisiana.* Louisiana State Department of Education, 1924.

BRESLICH, ERNST RUDOLPH AND OTHERS. "Supervision and Administration of Practice Teaching." In *Educational Administration and Supervision*, vol. 11, pp. 1-12, 1925.

CENTENNIAL CONFERENCE ON TEACHER-TRAINING. *Proceedings.* Indiana State Normal School, Indianapolis, Bulletin, 1923, vol. 17, No. 1.

CHARTERS, WERRETT WALLACE AND WAPLES, DOUGLAS. *The Commonwealth Teacher Training Study.* Chicago, University of Chicago Press, 1929.

CHILDS, H. G. *The Results of Practice Teaching on Teaching Efficiency.* U. S. Bureau of Education. Bulletin, 1917, No. 29.

COLVIN, STEPHEN SHELDON. "The Lesson Plan and Its Value to the Student Teacher." In *National Society for the Study of Education Yearbook* 18, Part I, pp. 190-212.

COOK, WILLIAM ADELBERT. *High School Observation and Practice.* Supervisor's edition. Baltimore, Warwick and York, 1925.

COOK, WILLIAM ADELBERT. "Introducing the Student to Practice Teaching." In *Educational Administration and Supervision*, vol. 10, pp. 294-302, 1924.

DAVIS, CALVIN OLIN. *Junior High School Education.* Yonkers, N. Y., World Book Co., 1924.

EVENDEN, EDWARD SAMUEL. "Cooperation of Teachers of Academic Subjects with the Training School." In *Educational Administration and Supervision*, vol. 11, pp. 307-319, 1925.

FELMLEY, DAVID F. AND OTHERS. "The Relation between Theory and Practice in the Training of Teachers." In *National Society for the Study of Education Yearbook*, vol. 2, Part II, pp. 548-555.

FLOWERS, JOHN GARLAND. "Experimentation in the Training Schools of Teachers Colleges." In *Texas Outlook*, 1927.

FLOWERS, JOHN GARLAND. *The Observation of Teaching.* Dallas, Southern Publishing Co., 1927.

GARRISON, NOBLE LEE. Current Practice in Coordination of College and Training School Work. The Author, Ypsilanti, Mich., 1931.

GARRISON, NOBLE LEE. *Status and Work of the Training Supervisors.* Contributions to Education, No. 280. New York, Teachers College, Columbia University, 1927.

GORDY, JOHN PANCOAST. *Rise and Growth of the Normal School Idea in the United States.* U. S. Bureau of Education. Circular No. 8, 1891.

HALL-QUEST, ALFRED LAWRENCE. *Professional Secondary Education in Teachers Colleges.* Contributions to Education, No. 169. New York, Teachers College, Columbia University, 1925.

HANUS, PAUL HENRY. "The Professional Preparation of High School Teachers." In *N.E.A. Proceedings*, 1907, pp. 563-577.

HENDERSON, JOSEPH LINDSEY. *The Distribution of a Student Teacher's Time.* University of Texas, Bulletin, No. 1858, 1918.

HILL, J. A. "The Development of Teachers Colleges." In *N.E.A. Proceedings*, 1925, pp. 394-402.

HILL, L. B. *Score Card for Practice Teachers and Teachers in Service.* National Society of College Teachers of Education, Educational Monographs, No. 9, pp. 10-12. 1920.

HUTSON, PERCIVAL W. Training of the High School Teachers of Minnesota. Bulletin, vol. 26, No. 46, College of Education, Educational Monographs No. 3. University of Minnesota, 1923.

INGLIS, ALEXANDER. *Principles of Secondary Education.* Boston, Houghton Mifflin Co., 1918.

JONES, LANCE GEORGE. *The Training of Teachers in England and Wales.* London, Oxford University Press, 1923.

KANDEL, ISAAC LEON. *History of Secondary Education.* Boston, Houghton Mifflin Co., 1931.

KOOS, LEONARD VINCENT. *The American Secondary School.* New York, Ginn and Co., 1927.

LEARNED, WILLIAM SITCHEL, BAGLEY, WILLIAM CHANDLER, AND OTHERS. *Professional Preparation of Teachers for American Public Schools.* New York, Carnegie Foundation for the Advancement of Teaching, Bulletin No. 14.

MEAD, ARTHUR RAYMOND. *Supervised Student Teaching.* Richmond, Johnson Publishing Company, 1930.

PAYNE, BRUCE RYBURN. "Twenty Years of Progress in Service Rendered by Normal Schools and Teachers Colleges." In *N.E.A. Proceedings*, 1928. Pp. 917ff.

PEIRCE, CLARENCE ANDREW AND CARVER, W. B., COMPS. *First State Normal School in America; Journals.* Harvard documents in the history of education, vol. 1. Harvard University Press, 1926.

PRYOR, HUGH CLARK. *Graded Units in Student Teaching.* Contributions to Education, No. 202. New York, Teachers College, Columbia University, 1926.

RANDOLPH, EDGAR DUNNINGTON. *The Professional Treatment of Subject Matter.* Baltimore, Warwick and York, 1924.

SEERLEY, HOMER HORATIO. "The Relation of Academic and Professional Work in a Normal School." In *N.E.A. Proceedings*, 1911, pp. 697-699.

SENSKA, NELLIE M. Making a "Detailed Score Card for Grading Student Teachers." In *Educational Administration and Supervision*, vol. 11, pp. 199-201, 1925.

SPRAGUE, HARRY A. "Coordination of Theory and Practice in Normal Schools." In *N.E.A. Proceedings*, 1918, pp. 212-214.

SPRAGUE, HARRY A. "Score Card for Rating Student Teachers in Training and Practice." In *Pedagogical Seminary*, vol. 24, pp. 72-80, March, 1917.

U. S. BUREAU OF EDUCATION. *Biennial Survey of Education, 1926-28.* U. S. Bureau of Education, Bulletin, 1930, No. 16, pp. 301-335.

WADE, N. A., AND FRETZ, R. M. "Some practices in the Administration and Supervision of Student Teaching." In *Educational Administration and Supervision*, vol. 12, pp. 124-130, 1926.

WAPLES, DOUGLAS. "A Device for the Student Teacher Conference." In *Educational Administration and Supervision*, vol. 10, pp. 564-567, 1924.

WILKINSON, WILLIAM ALBERT. "Functions and Organization of Practice Teaching in State Normal Schools." In *Educational Administration and Supervision*, vol. 4, pp. 289-296, 1918.

WILLIAMS, E. I. F. "Administration of Observation in the Teacher-Training Institutions of the United States." In *Educational Administration and Supervision*, vol. 8, pp. 331-342, 1922.

WILSON, LESTER M. *The Training Departments in the State Normal Schools in the United States.* Charleston, Ill., Eastern State Teachers College. Bulletin No. 66, 1919.